RAPTURE

POST-TRIBULATION AND PRE-WRATH

RAPTURE

POST-TRIBULATION AND PRE-WRATH

Don Montgomery

What Others Are Saying about RAPTURE: Post-Tribulation and Pre-Wrath

"Without exaggerating, this . . . [is] one of the most fascinating, insightful and original works. . . . It should be required reading . . . of last-days prophecy. I love it!"
—*Editor of a Christian Publication and Author of Christian Books*

"I shall not hesitate to recommend it to anyone I meet who wishes information on the subject."
—*Professor Emeritus*

"We appreciate your position, which is a wake-up call for the church."
—*Representative for the Author of Related Books*

". . . you have done much careful research and independent thinking. . . . Some fresh suggestions that I have never before heard and which certainly need to be thought about."
—*Professor of Biblical Studies*

". . . your excellent book . . . was just forwarded to me. Bravo! I wish you well with your worthy and well-written book."
—*Author of Related Books*

". . . I am sure it will be exceedingly helpful to the cause of Christ in the understanding of prophetic truth."
—*Author of a Related Book*

"The sentence structure is excellent for the complex material, and the organization leads one easily through the maze."
—*Author of Christian Poetry*

Printed in the United States of America

Packaged by WinePress Publishing, PO Box 428, Enumclaw, WA 98022. The views expressed or implied in this work do not necessarily reflect those of WinePress Publishing. Ultimate design, content and editorial accuracy of this work are the responsibilities of the author.

To contact the author, write to Don Montgomery, PO Box 908, Rochester, WA 98579.

All Scripture quotations are from the King James Version.

ISBN 1-57921-227-1
Library of Congress Catalog Card Number: 99-63455

Acknowledgments

This book would not have been accomplished without dear friends who prayed and helped proofread. And special help was provided by the dear ladies Carol Bogue and Cle Montgomery, who typed, retyped and retyped several more times! GOD bless them!

Contents

Description

The basic premise of this book centers upon two prophecies of a seven-year period in Daniel 9:25–27. These two prophecies have invariably been considered to be referencing the same period: the Seven Years of Tribulation. The premise presented is that the prophecies consist of two overlapping, partially concurrent seven-year periods.

One seven-year period is Jacob's Trouble, and there is probable agreement to its identification. The other period is a seven-year *covenant* allowing sacrifices, but the provisions for sacrifices are nullified at midterm. The remainder of this second prophecy describes activities within Jacob's Trouble, thereby indicating that the latter portion is during, or coincident, with Jacob's Trouble.

The result is a total, prophetic time period longer than seven years that provides for charting eighteen prophecies given in Daniel and Revelation and that contain specific timings for events and activities.

Harmonization of the eighteen prophetic time periods and events becomes relatively simple to provide a complete overview of GOD's plan about His timing to gather the Saints (Rapture) and His return to earth for His 1000-year reign on earth. Note: Twenty-three time prophecies are reviewed, but not all are included on charts—one prophecy occurs in Heaven, and the others relate to the fall of Babylon.

The Rapture occurs at the end of Great Tribulation and before GOD's Wrath: hence, *RAPTURE: Post-Tribulation and Pre-Wrath.*

No dates are suggested.

This book also contains point-by-point responses to some of the other Rapture concepts.

Short analyses are presented of some Scripture that may be descriptions of other events related to the identified timing plan. These are, admittedly, conjectural.

Potential readers are encouraged to read (with prayer) Chapter One before allowing previous beliefs to influence consideration of *RAPTURE: Post-Tribulation and Pre-Wrath.*

All quotations of Scripture are from the Authorized King James Version, and all underlines in those quotations have been added by the writer.

Use of *italics* and Scripture passages in the text are not necessarily direct quotations. Often, paraphrasing is utilized. Throughout, especially in the charts, a *year* is defined as 360 days.

Preface

Why have I written a book such as *RAPTURE: Post-Tribulation and Pre-Wrath*? A few years after realizing God is the Creator and acknowledging Lord Jesus Christ as my Lord and Saviour, I became deeply concerned that most teachings of the Rapture are contributing to a false hope about the *Blessed Hope*—fulfilled by the Rapture itself. The popular version of the Rapture is that believers will be *caught up* and taken from the earth prior to apocalyptic events that lead to the return and reign of Lord Jesus Christ on earth:

> I Thessalonians 4
> 17 Then we which are alive *and* remain shall be caught up together with them in the clouds, to meet the Lord in the air: and so shall we ever be with the Lord.

I have found no Scriptural evidence of a Rapture whereby believers will be taken from the earth prior to the Tribulation or Great Tribulation. Scripture seems to indicate quite the opposite, and my concern relates to Scripture passages such as:

> Matthew 24
> 12 And because iniquity shall abound, the love of many shall wax cold.

> II Thessalonians 2
> 3 Let no man deceive you by any means: for *that day shall not come,* except there come a falling away first, and that man of sin be revealed, the son of perdition;

> I Timothy 4
> 1 Now the Spirit speaketh expressly, that in the latter times

some shall depart from the faith, giving heed to seducing spirits, and doctrines of devils;

The flesh is *weak* (Matt. 26:14; Mark 14:38), and contemplation of events shortly before the return of Lord Jesus Christ can be emotional, apprehensive, and disturbing. Very briefly, we need to remember the words of Jesus Christ concerning tomorrow and His coming:

MATTHEW 6
34 Take therefore no thought for the morrow: for the morrow shall take thought for the things of itself. Sufficient unto the day *is* the evil thereof.

LUKE 12
37 Blessed *are* those servants, whom the lord when he cometh shall find watching: verily I say unto you, that he shall gird himself, and make them to sit down to meat, and will come forth and serve them.

When end-time events descend upon the world, Scripture will be fulfilled and "some shall depart from the faith . . . fall away. . . . the love of many shall wax cold". It's also sad to think this could be compounded by a loss of faith in church leadership and teachers who have held to a Rapture that precedes end-time events.

RAPTURE: Post-Tribulation and Pre-Wrath is not expected to be well received. It treads on too many toes, egos and entrenched ideas. This is well known from previous reactions and comments—heresy not even being the worst!

I confess that it has been those previous experiences that have kept this documentation from being attempted for over twelve years. The delay has been far too long. Let Scripture speak to anyone "that hath an ear" and "let him hear".

If the presented premise, evidence, and analyses are correct, or more accurate than other teachings, thank GOD! I ask Him only that He—the Father, His Son Lord Jesus Christ and His Holy Spirit—be glorified in accordance with His will! Amen!

This revised version has no changes to the basic concepts previously presented. The original version had discussions that needed better organization and application, but hopefully all these have been corrected. Also, some additions have been included to further corroborate the main issues presented.

Very little in either version is known to be published elsewhere. If that has happened, sincere apologies are extended. No literature search, per se, has been conducted. The prime search has been in Scripture with the aid of a few reference books. Where related materials have been found through casual reading of a few books and articles, they have been identified to the best of my ability.

Chapter One

1. Introduction

The word *Rapture* is not in English translations of Scripture; it is from a Latin word. *Rapture* means "being carried away in body or spirit" or "being carried away with joy and love". Usage of *Rapture* combines all of those when referring to Scripture passages of *snatch away, catch away, take away, gather together, transform* or *change* with the result of eternal joy in God's presence:

Snatch or Catch Away

I Thessalonians 4
17 Then we which are alive and remain shall be caught up together with them in the clouds, to meet the Lord in the air: and so shall we ever be with the Lord.

Taken Away or Received

Genesis 5
24 And Enoch walked with God: and he *was* not; for God took him.

Matthew 24
40 Then shall two be in the field; the one shall be taken, and the other left.

John 14
3 And if I go and prepare a place for you, I will come again, and receive you unto myself; that where I am, *there* ye may be also.

Gathering Together

II THESSALONIANS 2
[1] Now we beseech you, brethren, by the coming of our Lord Jesus Christ, and *by* our gathering together unto him,

MATTHEW 24
[31] And he shall send his angels with a great sound of a trumpet, and they shall gather together his elect from the four winds, from one end of heaven to the other.

Transform or Change

I CORINTHIANS 15
[52] In a moment, in the twinkling of an eye, at the last trump: for the trumpet shall sound, and the dead shall be raised incorruptible, and we shall be changed.

The idea expressed by *Rapture* is when GOD will *catch, take, receive, translate* and *gather* the changed believers in the clouds with Himself without the believers experiencing physical death on earth. This is the meaning of *Rapture* used in this writing.

Enoch was Raptured (mentioned previously) and so was Elijah:

II KINGS 2
[11] And it came to pass, as they still went on, and talked, that, behold, *there appeared* a chariot of fire, and horses of fire, and parted them both asunder; and Elijah went up by a whirlwind into heaven.

Most of the Scripture quotes given previously tell of a Rapture that is yet to occur. Popular belief is this Rapture will be prior to any of the apocalyptic events leading to the return and reign of Lord Jesus Christ on earth for 1000 years (Rev. 20:4, 7). The apocalyptic events are supposed to occur in a seven-year time period called *Tribulation*. Believers are expected to be Raptured from earth prior to the Tribulation, and this idea is called a *pre-Tribulation Rapture.*

Scripture contains many specified prophetic time periods. Attempts to place these into a seven-year period (Tribulation) have not been successful and usually ignore some of the specified time periods. Removing the time constraint of seven years would solve the problem, and this constraint does not appear to have been justified!

The seven-year period has been assumed to be described twice in Scripture (Dan. 9:25–27). This Seven-Year Tribulation is to start with a *covenant* and then end when Lord Jesus Christ returns to earth at Armageddon. But, the two descriptions include incompatible events and should not be considered the same seven-year period.

2. Seven Years of Tribulation?

If two descriptions for a *week* (seven years) are characterized by different events, then they really are not likely to be the same time periods but relate to different *weeks*.

First Description

One seven-year period is the remaining *week* (a week of years equals seven years) of the seventy weeks given to Daniel in a vision to answer his prayer. His prayer was to know the truth about Jeremiah's prophecy of seventy years in desolation of Jerusalem:

> JEREMIAH 25
> [11] And this whole land shall be a desolation, *and* an astonishment; and these nations shall serve the king of Babylon seventy years.

These *seventy years* were the exile of Judah to Babylon. Daniel was there. His prayer (Dan. 9:4–19) included concerns about the future of Jerusalem, Judah and all Israel:

DANIEL 9
2 In the first year of his reign, I Daniel understood by books
the number of the years, whereof the word of the LORD came
to Jeremiah the prophet, that he would accomplish seventy
years in the desolations of Jerusalem.
16 O Lord, according to all thy righteousness, I beseech thee,
let thine anger and thy fury be turned away from thy city
Jerusalem, thy holy mountain: because for our sins, and for
the iniquities of our fathers, Jerusalem and thy people *are
become* a reproach to all *that are* about us.
18 O my God, incline thine ear, and hear; open thine eyes,
and behold our desolations, and the city which is called
by thy name: for we do not present our supplications before
thee for our righteousness, but for thy great mercies.
19 O Lord, hear; O Lord, forgive; O Lord, hearken and do;
defer not, for thine own sake, O my God: for thy city and
thy people are called by thy name.

Daniel learned that the total time for Israel and Jerusalem was to be an additional seventy weeks (seventy weeks of years: 70 x 7 years):

DANIEL 9
24 Seventy weeks are determined upon thy people and upon
thy holy city, to finish the transgression, and to make an
end of sins, and to make reconciliation for iniquity, and to
bring in everlasting righteousness, and to seal up the vision
and prophecy, and to anoint the most Holy.

He was also told the number of years (weeks) to when Jesus Christ (Messiah) would be "cut off". That is now considered history, and there is *one* week of years that has not been fulfilled. This one final week is referred to as *Jacob's Trouble*:

DANIEL 9
25 Know therefore and understand, *that* from the going forth
of the commandment to restore and to build Jerusalem,
unto the Messiah the Prince, *shall be* seven weeks, and three

score and two weeks: the street shall be built again, and
the wall, even in troublous times.
26 And after threescore and two weeks shall Messiah be
cut off, but not for himself: and the people of the prince
that shall come shall destroy the city and the sanctuary;
and the end thereof *shall be* with a flood, and unto the end
of the war desolations are determined.

The history of Jerusalem before the exile to Babylon is described briefly here:

II Chronicles 36
17 Therefore he brought upon them the king of the Chaldees,
who slew their young men with the sword in the house of
their sanctuary, and had no compassion upon young man
or maiden, old man, or him that stooped for age: he gave
them all into his hand.
18 And all the vessels of the house of God, great and small,
and the treasures of the house of the Lord, and the treasures
of the king, and of his princes; all *these* he brought to
Babylon.
19 And they burnt the house of God, and brake down the
wall of Jerusalem, and burnt all the palaces thereof with
fire, and destroyed all the goodly vessels thereof.
20 And them that had escaped from the sword carried he
away to Babylon; where they were servants to him and
his sons until the reign of the kingdom of Persia:
21 To fulfil the word of the Lord by the mouth of Jeremiah,
until the land had enjoyed her sabbaths: *for* as long as she
lay desolate she kept sabbath, to fulfil threescore and ten
years.

This history and Daniel's prayer contain descriptions relating to *desolation, wickedness, no compassion, plunder, burning, destruction, confusion, great evil* and (God's) *fury*. The final week of seven years can be expected to be more of the same and worse, if possible. For this week of Jacob's Trouble, there are various descriptions throughout Scripture that are summarized in Ezekiel 7 and in:

JEREMIAH 30
[5] For thus saith the LORD; We have heard a voice of
trembling, of fear, and not of peace.
[6] Ask ye now, and see whether a man doth travail with
child? wherefore do I see every man with his hands on his
loins, as a woman in travail, and all faces are turned into
paleness?
[7] Alas! for that day *is* great, so that none *is* like it: it *is* even
the time of Jacob's trouble; but he shall be saved out of it.

This seven-year period of Jacob's Trouble will truly be of extreme hardships and trouble for Jerusalem, Judah, Israel and Jews everywhere. Many people of all nations will perish during the end times, but Israel will be punished hardest—only a *remnant* (trace) will be left:

ISAIAH 10
[20] And it shall come to pass in that day, *that* the remnant of
Israel, and such as are escaped of the house of Jacob, shall
no more again stay upon him that smote them; but shall
stay upon the LORD, the Holy One of Israel, in truth.
[22] For though thy people Israel be as the sand of the sea, *yet*
a remnant of them shall return: the consumption decreed
shall overflow with righteousness.
[23] For the Lord GOD of hosts shall make a consumption,
even determined, in the midst of all the land.

Second Description

A second description for a seven-year week has two parts: the first part has a specified time period from *confirm the covenant* until the *sacrifice and oblation cease:*

DANIEL 9
[27] And he shall confirm the covenant with many for one
week: and in the midst of the week he shall cause the
sacrifice and the oblation to cease, and for the
overspreading abominations he shall make *it* desolate,
even until the consummation, and that determined shall
be poured upon the desolate.

The first part of this week should be quite good for Israel—there will be worship, sacrifices and oblations which have been missing for over 1900 years. But, even though these years will start favorably for Israel *(peace and safety),* the situation will degenerate as the antichrist gains influence and power, and GOD rejects the *feasts and offerings:*

> I THESSALONIANS 5
> 3 For when they shall say, Peace and safety; then sudden destruction cometh upon them, as travail upon a woman with child; and they shall not escape.

> AMOS 5
> 18 Woe unto you that desire the day of the LORD! To what end *is* it for you? the day of the LORD *is* darkness, and not light.
> 19 As if a man did flee from a lion, and a bear met him; or went into the house, and leaned his hand on the wall, and a serpent bit him.
> 20 *Shall* not the day of the LORD *be* darkness, and not light? even very dark, and no brightness in it?
> 21 I hate, I despise your feast days, and I will not smell in your solemn assemblies.
> 22 Though ye offer me burnt offerings and your meat offerings, I will not accept *them:* neither will I regard the peace offerings of your fat beasts.

The first part of this second description of sacrifices and peace (implied) simply does not match the descriptions of Jacob's Trouble and should not be considered the same time period.

In other words, the second description (which is usually interpreted to be seven years of Jacob's Trouble) cannot be seven years of Jacob's Trouble, because the first three and one-half years of the seven years of Jacob's Trouble would have no *trouble!*

The described weeks simply cannot be the same weeks, but they have been considered the same time period, called a *Seven-Year Tribulation!*

It turns out that the two weeks must overlap. The second part of the *covenant week* (Dan. 9:27) has events that do match Jacob's Trouble: "desolation and abominations continue . . . until the consummation [completion of end times]". Completion of events after *sacrifice and oblation cessation* would not need to be confined to the remaining three and one-half years of the covenant: the *covenant* was broken and nullified. *Covenant* time would no longer be accountable.

The amount of overlap for these two weeks is not identified at this point, but Jacob's Trouble would start before the sacrifice and oblation are stopped: before the first three and one-half year period is completed. This should be expected. It will take major events to stop the sacrifice and oblation services: major events fitting the descriptions of Jacob's Trouble, Olivet Discourse, Revelation, etc.

The Major Points of View

- The descriptions of the *weeks* do not match, and thereby represent two different *weeks* (seven-year periods)
- Portions of the week descriptions include the same types of events, so portions of the time periods would be the same
- Overlap of portions of the seven-year periods means the overall time could not be confined to a total of seven years
- The prophetic time period from *confirmation of the covenant* until Lord Jesus Christ returns for His reign on earth will be longer than seven years

As a result, the terminology and usage of a Seven-Year Tribulation would appear difficult to defend; it does not mean what it is intended to mean.

3. Daniel's Overall Prophecy Timing

If the previously discussed seven-year time periods do not represent the same period but represent a longer time consisting of overlapping seven-year periods, what is the overall timing? How much does the time overlap?

Before looking for the answers to these questions, prophetic time periods need some definition. It is generally accepted that *weeks* represent seven-year periods (based on historical facts of Daniel's sixty-nine weeks) and are defined in:

GENESIS 29
27 Fulfil her week, and we will give thee this also for the service which thou shalt serve with me yet seven other years.

"Times, time and half a time" represent one half "week" and means three and one-half years. The three and one-half years are also represented by 42 months, or 1260 days:

REVELATION 12
6 And the woman fled into the wilderness, where she hath
a place prepared of God, that they should feed her there a
thousand two hundred *and* threescore days.
14 And to the woman were given two wings of a great eagle,
that she might fly into the wilderness, into her place, where
she is nourished for a time, and times, and half a time,
from the face of the serpent.

REVELATION 13
5 And there was given unto him a mouth speaking great things and blasphemies; and power was given unto him to continue forty *and* two months.

These are based on a 360-day year, not the 365-day year of current calendars. A week of years would be 2520 days—almost 37 days short of a current seven years.

Back to Daniel's prophecies: before learning of the covenant concerning sacrifices, Daniel had received an earlier vision about the sacrifices being taken away:

DANIEL 8
11 *Yea,* he magnified *himself* even to the prince of the host,

and by him the daily *sacrifice* was taken away, and the place
of his sanctuary was cast down.
13 Then I heard one saint speaking, and another saint said
unto that certain *saint* which spake, How long *shall be* the
vision *concerning* the daily *sacrifice,* and the transgression
of desolation, to give both the sanctuary and the host to be
trodden under foot?
14 And he said unto me, Unto two thousand and three
hundred days; then shall the sanctuary be cleansed.

So, Daniel had already known 2300 days would ensue from *sacrifice cessation* until the *sanctuary is cleansed:* basically, he knew the total time from the covenant confirmation to the sanctuary cleansing would be 3560 days (2300 + 1260 days).

CHART #1

DANIEL'S OVERALL PROPHECY TIMING

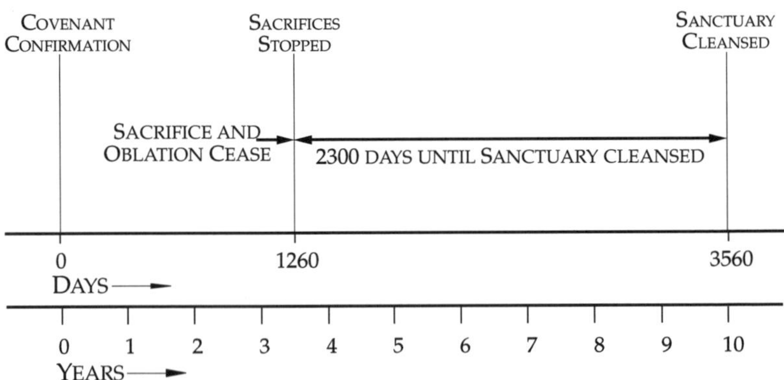

If Jacob's Trouble were to end with "sanctuary cleansing", it would start seven years previously (7 x 360 = 2520 days). Subtracting 2520 days from 3560 indicates Jacob's Trouble would start no later than 1040 days after the covenant confirmation, which would also be no later than 220 days before the sacrifice cessation.

However, the end of Jacob's Trouble cannot be equated to sanctuary cleansing. Image removal and physical cleansing along with some repair of the facilities, utensils and furnishings could be expected and would take some time. Additional time should also be expected for ceremonial activities and festivals associated with the cleansing.

Jacob's Trouble is expected to end no later than Armageddon. Lord Jesus Christ will return to earth first, apparently at Bozrah in Edom, and probably proceed to other locations on His way to Jerusalem:

> Isaiah 63
> [1] Who is this that cometh from Edom, with dyed garments from Bozrah? this *that is* glorious in his apparel, travelling in the greatness of his strength? I that speak in righteousness, mighty to save.
> [2] Wherefore *art thou* red in thine apparel, and thy garments like him that treadeth in the winevat?
> [3] I have trodden the winepress alone; and of the people *there was* none with me: for I will tread them in mine anger, and trample them in my fury; and their blood shall be sprinkled upon my garments, and I will stain all my raiment.

> Revelation 19
> [12] His eyes *were* as a flame of fire, and on his head *were* many crowns; and he had a name written, that no man knew, but he himself.
> [13] And he *was* clothed with a vesture dipped in blood: and his name is called The Word of God.
> [14] And the armies *which were* in heaven followed him upon white horses, clothed in fine linen, white and clean.

Presumably, He would take some days to reach Jerusalem. These events and those for cleansing would move the start and end of Jacob's Trouble to earlier times.

CHART #2

TIME OF JACOB'S TROUBLE

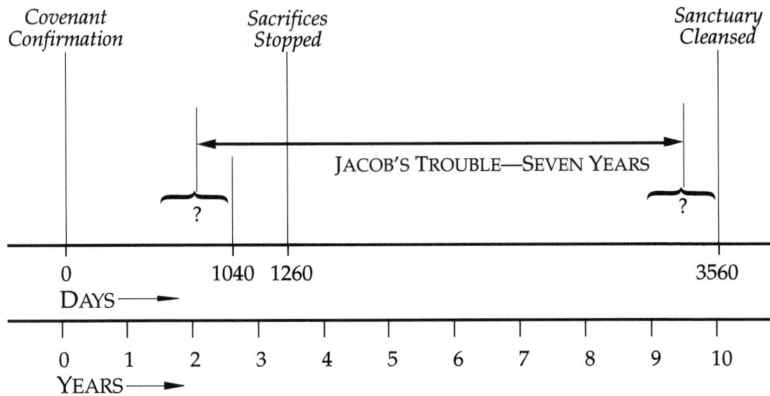

There is one major issue that could also change the preparation time prior to the sanctuary cleansing: whether a Temple would have to be built. For sacrifices to be offered, a Temple is expected, and presumably (but not for certain) would be available at the time of the covenant confirmation. A covenant to perform sacrifices does not mean a sanctuary will be ready. Or a *covenant sanctuary* may be in the wrong location. For example, prior to the exile to Babylon, Ahaz (king of Judah) had moved Temple utensils to Damascus and worshipped there after bribing enemies for peace in a covenant of lies and falsehood called "a covenant with death and with hell". (More about this covenant later: Isa. 28:1–21; II Kings 16:1–18).

Also, there are differing opinions whether Jesus Christ's words about Temple destruction have been fulfilled:

MATTHEW 24
1 Jesus went out, and departed from the temple: and his disciples came to *him* for to shew him the buildings of the temple.
2 And Jesus said unto them, See ye not all these things?

verily I say unto you, There shall not be left here one stone
upon another, that shall not be thrown down.

MARK 13
1 And as he went out of the temple, one of his disciples
saith unto him, Master, see what manner of stones and
what buildings *are here!*
2 And Jesus answering said unto him, Seest thou these great
buildings? there shall not be left one stone upon another,
that shall not be thrown down.

LUKE 21
5 And as some spake of the temple, how it was adorned
with goodly stones and gifts. he said,
6 *As for* these things which ye behold, the days will come,
in the which there shall not be left one stone upon another,
that shall not be thrown down.

The last Temple was destroyed in A.D. 70, but there are still some remains: the main items being some of the foundation which is called the Wailing Wall, and the East Gate which is closed off—until Jesus Christ returns! Has the prophecy been fulfilled? Does it apply to a new Temple of the end times?

The second part of Daniel 9:26 indicates "destruction of the city and the sanctuary":

DANIEL 9
26 And after threescore and two weeks shall Messiah be cut
off, but not for himself: and the people of the prince that
shall come shall destroy the city and the sanctuary; and the
end thereof *shall be* with a flood, and unto the end of the
war desolations are determined.

The term used for *destroy* means "corrupt, spoil, mar" and doesn't specifically indicate the people will *totally* destroy the sanctuary. If another sanctuary is to be built by human hands, significant time of months, or even years, could be required (Zech. 6:12–13, 15).

The above issues about the sanctuary cleansing are mentioned to emphasize the beginning and ending of Jacob's Trouble and can only be approximated at this point. It should be safe to indicate its start will be no later than 1040 days after the covenant confirmation.

The total time period from the covenant confirmation until the sanctuary cleansing seems to be clearly identified in Scripture as 3560 days. Obviously, it is believed the 3560-day interval is correct! And it then becomes relatively easy to identify many other time periods and events. The approach eliminates the many problems associated with trying to place prophetic time periods and events into one seven-year course of time.

4. Revealing of the Antichrist

Building upon the previously identified time periods and events provides a means for establishing additional events of prophecy. It is appropriate to identify when an *abomination of desolation* will "stand in the holy place". Once the daily sacrifice is taken away, there will be 1290 days until the abomination stands:

> DANIEL 12
> 11 And from the time *that* the daily *sacrifice* shall be taken away, and the abomination that maketh desolate set up, *there shall be* a thousand two hundred and ninety days.

> MATTHEW 24
> 15 When ye therefore shall see the abomination of desolation, spoken of by Daniel the prophet, stand in the holy place, (whoso readeth, let him understand,)

> MARK 13
> 14 But when ye shall see the abomination of desolation, spoken of by Daniel the prophet, standing where it ought not, (let him that readeth understand,) then let them that be in Judaea flee to the mountains:

This is 1260 plus 1290 days after the covenant is confirmed: 2550 days equals one month more than seven years.

CHART #3

ABOMINATION OF DESOLATION

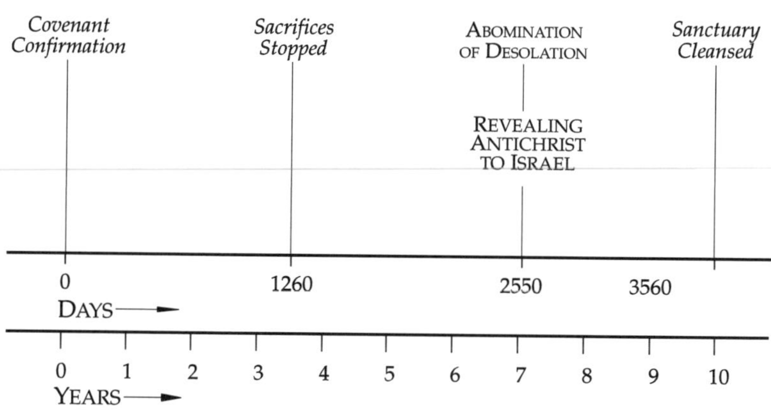

It would be well to notice that Daniel used the term *set up,* whereas Jesus Christ stated *stand* and *it.* Do these terms refer to the antichrist or to the image? Do they mean *set up* the image so it will *stand?*

> Revelation 13
> 15 And he had power to give life unto the image of the beast, that the image of the beast should both speak, and cause that as many as would not worship the image of the beast should be killed.

It appears to be the image. Daniel used the same term for *set up* in other instances:

> Daniel 9
> 10 Neither have we obeyed the voice of the Lord our God, to walk in his laws, which he set before us by his servants the prophets.

> Daniel 10
> 15 And when he had spoken such words unto me, I set my face toward the ground, and I became dumb.

In these cases, the thing *set* was placed in that position by one other than itself. Also, use of *stand* may refer to *stand still*, such as an image would be expected to do:

MATTHEW 2
[9] When they had heard the king, they departed; and, lo, the star, which they saw in the east, went before them, till it came and stood over where the young child was.

MATTHEW 6
[5] And when thou prayest, thou shalt not be as the hypocrites *are:* for they love to pray standing in the synagogues and in the corners of the streets, that they may be seen of men. Verily I say unto you, They have their reward.

MATTHEW 20
[32] Jesus stood still, and called them, and said, What will ye that I shall do unto you?

The terms used are not totally definitive, but the issue is presented for comparison to when the antichrist "sitteth in the temple" (i.e., holy of holies):

II THESSALONIANS 2
[1] Now we beseech you, brethren, by the coming of our Lord Jesus Christ, and *by* our gathering together unto him,
[2] That ye be not soon shaken in mind, or be troubled, neither by spirit, nor by word, nor by letter as from us, as that the day of Christ is at hand.
[3] Let no man deceive you by any means: for *that day shall not come*, except there come a falling away first, and that man of sin be revealed, the son of perdition;
[4] Who opposeth and exalteth himself above all that is called God, or that is worshipped; so that he as God sitteth in the temple of God, shewing himself that he is God.

The last verse shows the antichrist being seated when *sitteth* implies a different event than setting up an image to be worshipped. When the antichrist is seated, he is showing himself that he is GOD. Ugh!

Sitteth and *seat* indicate authority and some rest after completing something:

> MATTHEW 19
> [28] And Jesus said unto them, Verily I say unto you, That ye which have followed me, in the regeneration when the Son of man shall sit in the throne of his glory, ye also shall sit upon twelve thrones, judging the twelve tribes of Israel.

> MARK 16
> [19] So then, after the Lord had spoken unto them, he was received up into heaven, and sat on the right hand of God.

> REVELATION 3
> [21] To him that overcometh will I grant to sit with me in my throne, even as I also overcame, and am set down with my Father in his throne.

Setting up the abomination of desolation, and the antichrist sitting to show himself as GOD are likely to be separate events. These events probably occur very close together, such as in a single ceremony with the image being set up first.

II Thessalonians 2:1–4 seems to state very clearly that the Rapture—gathering together—will not occur until after the antichrist is revealed! The Rapture, then, could not occur until at least 2550 days have lapsed from *covenant confirmation*.

It is very disheartening to read, or hear statements such as: "Because the Scriptures teach that the Antichrist will not be revealed until after the Rapture of the church. . . "[1] This statement appears to be in direct opposition to the Scripture in II Thessalonians 2:1–4. It would seem wise to avoid such teaching!

Undoubtedly, the identity of the antichrist will be known to many who are aware of related Scripture. But, the *revealing* will be to the Jews. It should be remembered those prophecies are answering Daniel's prayer about Judah, Jerusalem, Israel, etc. Israel will not understand until the image is *set up*—standing in the holy place:

Isaiah 29
10 For the Lord hath poured out upon you the spirit of deep
sleep, and hath closed your eyes: the prophets and your
rulers, the seers hath he covered.
14 Therefore, behold, I will proceed to do a marvellous
work among this people, *even* a marvellous work and a
wonder: for the wisdom of their wise *men* shall perish,
and the understanding of their prudent *men* shall be hid.

Romans 11
7 What then? Israel hath not obtained that which he seeketh
for; but the election hath obtained it, and the rest were
blinded
8 (According as it is written, God hath given them the spirit
of slumber, eyes that they should not see, and ears that
they should not hear;) unto this day.

When the antichrist is revealed to the Jews, those in Judea are instructed *to flee:*

Matthew 24
15 When ye therefore shall see the abomination of
desolation, spoken of by Daniel the prophet, stand in the
holy place, (whoso readeth, let him understand,)
16 Then let them which be in Judaea flee into the mountains:
17 Let him which is on the housetop not come down to take
any thing out of his house:
18 Neither let him which is in the field return back to take
his clothes.

Mark 13
14 But when ye shall see the abomination of desolation,
spoken of by Daniel the prophet, standing where it ought
not, (let him that readeth understand,) then let them that
be in Judaea flee to the mountains:
15 And let him that is on the housetop not go down into the
house, neither enter *therein,* to take any thing out of his
house:

Instruction to flee is directed to those in Judea. Although Judea includes Jerusalem, it may (by then) be too late to flee from Jerusalem. Jews should be familiar with Daniel's prophecies and the history of previous, similar events that have occurred (Antiochus IV Epiphanes and Rome's Titus), but they are not likely to be familiar with the New Testament warnings.

> LUKE 21
> 21 Then let them which are in Judaea flee to the mountains;
> and let them which are in the midst of it depart out; and
> let not them that are in the countries enter thereinto.

Fleeing from Judea, desecration of the holy place, and (probably) the antichrist taking his seat are scheduled to be completed 2550 days after covenant confirmation.

Then, there will be: ". . . the coming of our Lord Jesus Christ, and by our gathering together unto him! . . ." Amen!

5. Resurrection and Rapture

Daniel was also informed when he would be resurrected:

> DANIEL 12
> 13 But go thou thy way till the end *be:* for thou shalt rest,
> and stand in thy lot at the end of the days.

He was told to rest and (then) stand at the end of the days.

There is the idea suggesting Daniel was being instructed to *stand firm* until the end of his days—until he died. Standing firm is one use of the translated term. However, a literal *stand,* or rising up, is used in other examples, such as:

> GENESIS 18
> 8 And he took butter, and milk, and the calf which he had
> dressed, and set *it* before them; and he stood by them under
> the tree, and they did eat.

DANIEL 1
[5] And the king appointed them a daily provision of the king's meat, and of the wine which he drank: so nourishing them three years, that at the end thereof they might <u>stand</u> before the king.

DANIEL 12
[5] Then I Daniel looked, and, behold, there <u>stood</u> other two, the one on this side of the bank of the river, and the other on that side of the bank of the river.

A *stand up* idea is more appropriate since he could not really rest and stand firm—rest and stand while he was dead. **<u>He was being told when he would be resurrected!</u>**

Resurrection would be at the *end of the days,* which refers back to the previous verse given below. The "go . . . till the end" is also referring to the same verse:

DANIEL 12
[12] <u>Blessed *is* he that waiteth,</u> and cometh to <u>the thousand three hundred and five and thirty days.</u>

Daniel had been told that he should go rest and (then) stand at the end of the days—be resurrected—which would occur at the 1335 days.

"Blessed is he that waiteth" applies to <u>all</u> Saints: both Old Testament and New Testament Believers!

This is the RAPTURE!

ISAIAH 30
[18] And therefore will the LORD wait, that he may be gracious unto you, and therefore will he be exalted, that he may have mercy upon you: for the LORD *is* a God of judgment: <u>blessed *are* all they that wait for him.</u>

TITUS 2
[13] Looking for that <u>blessed hope,</u> and the <u>glorious appearing of the great God and our Saviour Jesus Christ;</u>

So Daniel knew he would be resurrected at 1260 plus 1335 days (2595 total) after confirmation of the covenant! Then this must also be the timing of the *last trump:* the last day for any Believers (dead or alive) on earth!

> JOHN 6
> 44 No man can come to me, except the Father which hath sent me draw him: and I will raise him up at the last day.
>
> I CORINTHIANS 15
> 52 In a moment, in the twinkling of an eye, at the last trump: for the trumpet shall sound, and the dead shall be raised incorruptible, and we shall be changed.

In the Olivet Discourse, there is a verse indicating

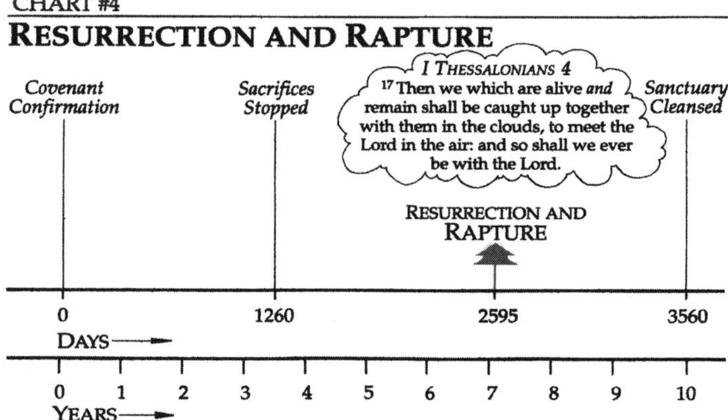

Believers may escape all these things: escape the end-time events. The escape could be used to mean a previous Rapture:

> LUKE 21
> 36 Watch ye therefore, and pray always, that ye may be accounted worthy to escape all these things that shall come to pass, and to stand before the Son of man.

The term used for *escape* is two combined words: *from* and *flee.*

Flee is the same used for instructing those in Judea to flee when the image, the abomination of desolation, is set up in the holy place (Matt. 24:15–16; Mark 13:14; Luke 21:20–21). The meaning is "flee from all these things". There would be no inference of *escaping* due to a previous Rapture.

The analysis of timing and events given to Daniel indicate the resurrection and Rapture will occur during periods of great distress. The timing will be 1260 days plus 1335 days (2595 days).

Once the date occurs for covenant confirmation, the number of days to resurrection and Rapture is identified to be 2595 days!

CHART #5

PRELIMINARY SUMMARY

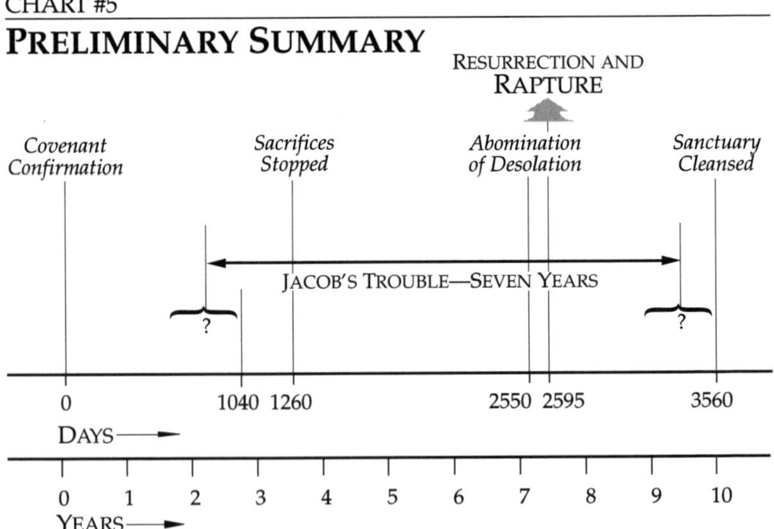

Chapter Two

6. Satan Cast to Earth

One of the many events apostle John witnessed in his Revelation visions was Satan being cast out of heaven and "unto the earth":

> REVELATION 12
> 12 Therefore rejoice, *ye* heavens, and ye that dwell in them. Woe to the inhabiters of the earth and of the sea! for the devil is come down unto you, having great wrath, because he knoweth that he hath but a short time.
> 13 And when the dragon saw that he was cast unto the earth, he persecuted the woman which brought forth the man *child*.

Satan has a wingding, tizzyfit temper tantrum and in "great wrath" attempts vengeance upon Israel—identified as "the woman fled" and also as "she might fly into the wilderness":

> REVELATION 12
> 6 And the woman fled into the wilderness, where she hath a place prepared of God, that they should feed her there a thousand two hundred *and* threescore days.
> 14 And to the woman were given two wings of a great eagle, that she might fly into the wilderness, into her place, where she is nourished for a time, and times, and half a time, from the face of the serpent.

For a long time, these two descriptions of the woman (Israel) going into the wilderness were held to be the same event, but they probably are different!

In the first instance, the "woman fled into the wilderness": she fled, ran away, escaped. In the second case, the "woman will fly". In all other Scripture usage, the term for *fly* refers to angels <u>*flying*</u> and does not mean *run away* nor *fled:*

> REVELATION 8
> [13] And I beheld, and heard an angel <u>flying</u> through the midst of heaven, saying with a loud voice, Woe, woe, woe, to the inhabiters of the earth by reason of the other voices of the trumpet of the three angels, which are yet to sound!

> REVELATION 14
> [6] And I saw another angel <u>fly</u> in the midst of heaven, having the everlasting gospel to preach unto them that dwell on the earth, and to every nation, and kindred, and tongue, and people,

When Satan is cast to earth, Israel (a portion, the *remnant)* "will fly into her place in the wilderness". That will occur through some supernatural means, as indicated by the "two wings of a great eagle"—probably Michael (Dan. 12:1)—and protected from the serpent, who is Satan.

Satan pursues the woman who is helped by supernatural means—which was foreshadowed by Israel's escape from Pharaoh when the water was parted. This time the water is *swallowed up*:

> REVELATION 12
> [15] And the <u>serpent cast</u> out of his mouth water as <u>a flood after the woman,</u> that he might cause her to be carried away of the flood.
> [16] And the earth helped the woman; and the earth opened her mouth, and <u>swallowed up the flood</u> which the dragon cast out of his mouth.

Because the woman is being nourished in the wilderness, Satan goes to make war with the remainder of her children, the Believers:

> REVELATION 12
> [17] And the dragon was wroth with the woman, and went to make war with the remnant of <u>her seed</u>, which keep the commandments of God, and have the <u>testimony of Jesus Christ</u>.

Believers like the apostle John and the Lord's angel (probably Gabriel), have the "testimony of Jesus Christ":

REVELATION 1
2 Who bare record of the word of God, and of the testimony of Jesus Christ, and of all things that he saw.

REVELATION 19
10 And I fell at his feet to worship him. And he said unto me, See *thou do it* not: I am thy fellowservant, and of thy brethren that have the testimony of Jesus: worship God: for the testimony of Jesus is the spirit of prophecy.

Testimony means testimony: bearing witness, testifying, certifying, statements of knowledge—the duties of Believers. Believers have the testimony of Jesus Christ! So, Believers will be on earth until sometime after Satan is cast to earth, and they will be attacked by Satan with war!

The timing of Satan being cast to earth can be no later than when he attempts to persecute the woman who is carried away and nourished for a "time, times, and half a time". This would be no later than 2300 days (3560 less 1260) from covenant confirmation.

CHART #6

SATAN CAST TO EARTH

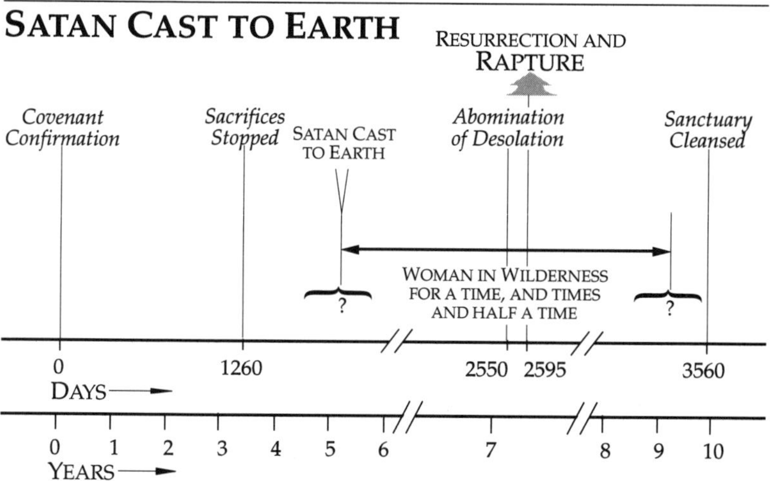

Now back to the woman when she *flees* into the wilderness—not carried by supernatural means. This happens before Satan is cast from heaven. There are two different wilderness locations: one is "a place prepared of GOD" that she flees into, and the other location is her place where "she is taken".

Israel (a remnant—more likely a remnant of Judah) is in the first wilderness for a "thousand two hundred and threescore days", and in the second wilderness for a "time, times, and half a time". These add up to the seven years of Jacob's Trouble—a seven-year period when GOD will protect a remnant of Israel (see chart 7).

Fleeing Judea when the abomination of desolation is brought to "stand in the holy place" (Matt. 24:15) "where it ought not" (Mark 13:14) should not be equated with the woman having either *fled* or *might fly* into the wildernesses. Jesus Christ's narrative is about anybody in Judea—those "in Judea . . . on housetop . . . in the field . . . flee into the mountains" (Matt. 24:16–18; Mark 13:14–15). Jesus Christ is saying get out of Judea! Later, it becomes apparent this will occur during the sixth sounding of the angel (Sixth Trumpet) and "the third part of men" will be slain (Rev. 9:18).

CHART #7

ISRAEL'S REMNANT IN WILDERNESSES

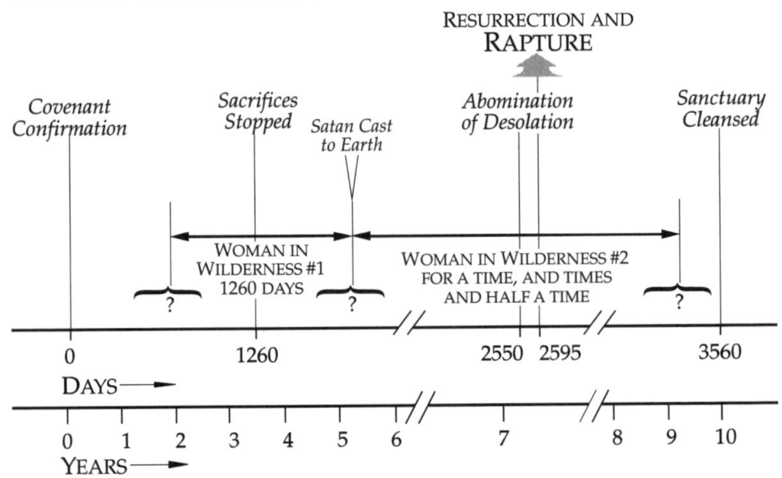

The eyes and understanding of Israel will still be hidden from truth when Satan comes to earth! The eyes and understanding of many (others) will be open. It is likely that the image and the two beasts may have their worship and ceremonies prior to abomination of desolation, but this would occur at some other location(s). The main story revolves around an unbelieving Israel.

7. God's Two Witnesses

In apostle John's visions of Revelation, he learned of GOD's *Two Witnesses* who will prophesy for 1260 days:

> REVELATION 11
> [3] And I will give *power* unto my two witnesses, and they shall prophesy a thousand two hundred *and* threescore days, clothed in sackcloth.

These Two Witnesses have a testimony that, although not stated, must be the same testimony previously mentioned and given elsewhere (Rev. 1:2; 12–17; 19:10): the testimony of Jesus Christ. They are also Believers, just as the apostle John and the Lord's angel:

> REVELATION 11
> [7] And when they shall have finished their testimony, the beast that ascendeth out of the bottomless pit shall make war against them, and shall overcome them, and kill them.

The witnessing and testimony (also miracles) occurs during the Tribulation and into the time period after Satan is cast to earth. Most of their witnessing and prophesying is when the Beast is in power.

Daniel had been told there would be three and one-half years to accomplish certain events:

> DANIEL 12
> [7] And I heard the man clothed in linen, which *was* upon

the waters of the river, when he held up his right hand and his left hand unto heaven, and sware by him that liveth for ever that *it shall be* for a time, times, and an half; and when he shall have accomplished to scatter the power of the holy people, all these *things* shall be finished.

The "accomplished" events would include the antichrist making his place on the holy mountain (Jerusalem), scattering power of the holy people, the first resurrection and the Rapture:

Daniel 11
45 And he shall plant the tabernacles of his palace between the seas in the glorious holy mountain; yet he shall come to his end, and none shall help him.

Daniel 12
1 And at that time shall Michael stand up, the great prince which standeth for the children of thy people: and there shall be a time of trouble, such as never was since there was a nation *even* to that same time: and at that time thy people shall be delivered, every one that shall be found written in the book.

The statement "these things shall be finished" refers to the deliverances, but they will not happen until it has been "accomplished to scatter the power of the holy people". These Two Witnesses certainly are *holy* people, and they will have their power scattered.

All other Believers must also await a scattering of power—usually considered removal of the Holy Spirit, but nowhere so identified (see References 2, 3, 4 for probable explanations). Also, it should be noted that the term is *scatter,* not *removal*!

Then Resurrection and Rapture into the Clouds of Heaven!

Revelation 1
7 Behold, he cometh with clouds; and every eye shall see

him, and they *also* which pierced him: and all kindreds of the earth shall wail because of him. Even so, Amen.

I THESSALONIANS 4
16 For the Lord himself shall descend from heaven with a shout, with the voice of the archangel, and with the trump of God: and the dead in Christ shall rise first:
17 Then we which are alive *and* remain shall be caught up together with them in the clouds, to meet the Lord in the air: and so shall we ever be with the Lord.

MATTHEW 24
30 And then shall appear the sign of the Son of man in heaven: and then shall all the tribes of the earth mourn, and they shall see the Son of man coming in the clouds of heaven with power and great glory.

Also see: Matthew 26:64; Mark 13:26–27; Luke 21:27; Acts 1:9; I Corinthians 15:51–52; Revelation 14:14–16.

All Believers/Saints should be resurrected or Raptured at the same time. With the Two Witnesses having power for 1260 days ending three and one-half days prior to resurrection and Rapture, their start of prophesying would be the seventy-first day after sacrifices are stopped.

CHART #8

GOD'S TWO WITNESSES

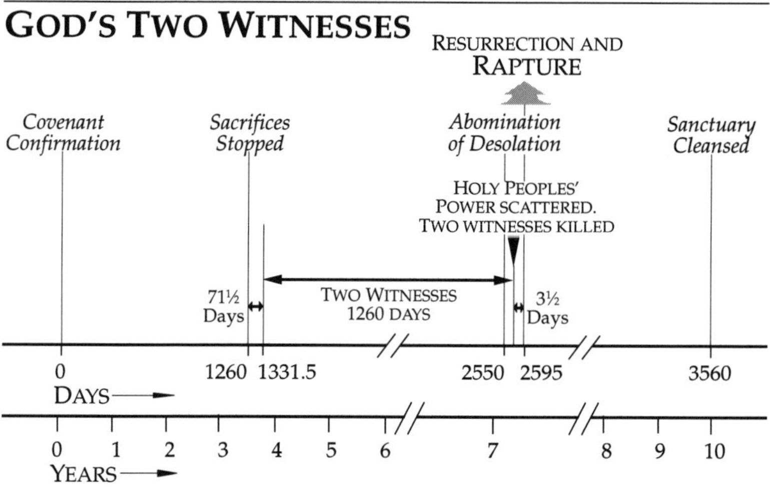

It should be noticed that once the Two Witnesses are killed, there will be many people who see their bodies:

REVELATION 11
9 And they of the people and kindreds and tongues and nations shall see their dead bodies three days and an half, and shall not suffer their dead bodies to be put in graves.

And, these people will have parties of celebration:

REVELATION 11
10 And they that dwell upon the earth shall rejoice over them, and make merry, and shall send gifts one to another; because these two prophets tormented them that dwelt on the earth.

But when the Two Witnesses are resurrected, these same people will have great fear when they see the resurrected witnesses, and "they heard a great voice from heaven". Then the Two Witnesses ascend to the clouds, as do the other Saints:

REVELATION 11
11 And after three days and an half the spirit of life from God entered into them, and they stood upon their feet; and great fear fell upon them which saw them.
12 And they heard a great voice from heaven saying unto them, Come up hither. And they ascended up to heaven in a cloud; and their enemies beheld them.

If there had been a previous resurrection and Rapture, would all these people react the way they do? It doesn't seem too likely does it?

Chapter Three

8. Doctrine of Imminency

The idea of knowing when the Rapture will occur can be considered contrary to a *doctrine of imminency*, which indicates Rapture timing cannot be known in advance. In other words, Rapture timing cannot be known in advance because Lord Jesus Christ's Coming should be expected at any time. This tends toward circular reasoning, which is not likely to be Scriptural.

Imminency is Scriptural in relation to the individual; it is a message to all on an individual basis. Each of the letters to the seven churches contain the same basic message to individuals: "He that hath an ear, let him hear what the Spirit saith" (Rev. 2:7, 11, 17, 29; 3:6, 13, 22 and similarly in Rev. 13:9). Just as salvation is on an individual basis (Phil. 2:12), so it is when each individual's time ends on this earth:

> ECCLESIASTES 3
> [1] To every *thing there is* a season, and a time to every purpose under the heaven:
> [2] A time to be born, and a time to die; a time to plant, and a time to pluck up *that which is* planted;

> ECCLESIASTES 8
> [8] *There is* no man that hath power over the spirit to retain the spirit; neither *hath he* power in the day of death: and *there is* no discharge in *that* war; neither shall wickedness deliver those that are given to it.

Evidently, the idea of knowing a date or time of the resurrection and Rapture is considered dangerous because

Believers may be tempted to backslide until just before the end-time events occur. Believers would backslide into spiritual sleep, thus neglecting their duties to God and each other. Scripture has many warnings about proper attitude and behavior, because no individual knows their own future:

Luke 12
17 And he thought within himself, saying, What shall I do,
because I have no room where to bestow my fruits?
18 And he said, This will I do: I will pull down my barns,
and build greater; and there will I bestow all my fruits and
my goods.
19 And I will say to my soul, Soul, thou hast much goods
laid up for many years; take thine ease. eat, drink, *and* be
merry.
20 But God said unto him, *Thou* fool, this night thy soul shall
be required of thee: then whose shall those things be, which
thou hast provided?

James 4
14 Whereas ye know not what *shall be* on the morrow. For
what *is* your life? It is even a vapour, that appeareth for a
little time, and then vanisheth away.

II Corinthians 5
8 We are confident, *I say*, and willing rather to be absent from
the body, and to be present with the Lord.
9 Wherefore we labour, that, whether present or absent we
may be accepted of him.
10 For we must all appear before the judgment seat of Christ;
that every one may receive the things *done* in *his* body,
according to that he hath done, whether *it be* good or bad.

Proverbs 27
1 Boast not thyself of tomorrow; for thou knowest not what
a day may bring forth.

Personal observation indicates a "secret" imminency of the Rapture turns many Believers away from studying and learning about the glorious Coming of Lord Jesus Christ—the biggest and most hoped for event there is for a Believer! The attitude becomes: "Why bother to learn or understand about the Coming of Lord Jesus Christ when it will happen suddenly, secretly, and before the antichrist causes any problems?" The idea of GOD's imminent (sudden, secret) removal of His people from earth prior to any Tribulation appears to be held primarily by one group: it ". . . will happen before *Americans* get persecuted, since in Central America jungles, Soviet Gulags, Chinese labor camps, Pakistani jails, Indian riots, and Sudanese villages countless believers have already paid the ultimate price for their faith. This teaching on the Rapture and persecution is currently a largely Western-oriented idea, and its teachers seem oblivious to the levels of suffering other Christians endure." (Quotation used by permission.)[5]

Why do so many pastors, teachers, and writers—directly or indirectly—discourage the study of end times and the summary given in the Book of Revelation? Such discouragement is directly contrary to GOD's desires expressed in Scripture!

The Book of Revelation has seven promises of blessings for Believers. These blessings are not the purpose of the promises—GOD simply shows how interested He is in having His Believers fully understand His end-time plans! The written Revelation of Jesus Christ starts and ends with blessing for those who read (or hear) and keep the Revelation prophecies. The Greek word for *keep* means to "keep an eye on, watch, or observe".

> REVELATION 1
> [3] Blessed *is* he that readeth, and they that hear the words of this prophecy, and keep those things which are written therein: for the time *is* at hand.

> REVELATION 22
> [7] Behold, I come quickly. Blessed *is* he that keepeth the sayings of the prophecy of this book.

The idea of watching or observing is reinforced even more in Revelation:

REVELATION 3
[3] Remember therefore how thou hast received and heard, and hold fast, and repent. If therefore thou shalt not watch, I will come on thee as a thief, and thou shalt not know what hour I will come upon thee.

REVELATION 16
[15] Behold, I come as a thief. Blessed *is* he that watcheth, and keepeth his garments, lest he walk naked, and they see his shame.

The Greek word translated (above) to "hold fast" is the same word previously translated to "keep" and also means "to watch".

There are four additional blessings relating to Believers who do His commandments, participate in the first resurrection, and are invited to the "marriage supper of the Lamb" (Rev. 14:13; 19:9; 20:6; 22:14).

Really, it simply is not appropriate to expect a secret, sudden (imminent) coming of Christ when Jesus Christ's own words instruct to keep watch and observe the events associated with His Coming (Rapture)!

9. Tribulation and Wrath Are Different!

A basic distinction should be established between the meaning of *Tribulation* and *Wrath*. Because they are different, there is the likelihood they represent different events and time frames during the end times.

- *Tribulation* is pressure, affliction, trial, and/or distress continuing over a period of time to try one's endurance and patience.
- *Wrath* is intense anger or action carried out in great anger, especially for punishment or vengeance.

Regardless of specific definitions, or source of definitions, *Tribulation* and *Wrath* are distinctly different. Just check any dictionary or lexicon!

During the past ten to fifteen years, the differences are becoming more recognized with some end-time concepts separating the two and placing the Rapture prior to a period of Wrath. Various times are identified for the start of Wrath; hence, various times have been identified for the Rapture. Such views are very close to the basic ideas presented in this book.

However, the most popular view presents the Rapture as occurring prior to Tribulation, or Great Tribulation periods. Associated Tribulation or Great Tribulation periods are considered only to be a seven-year period and the Tribulation and Wrath events are not separated. In the Olivet Discourse, Lord Jesus Christ talked about a Great Tribulation:

> MATTHEW 24
> 21 For then shall be great tribulation, such as was not since the beginning of the world to this time, no, nor ever shall be.

> MARK 13
> 19 For *in* those days shall be affliction, such as was not from the beginning of the creation which God created unto this time, neither shall be.

But, Jesus Christ also indicated an end to Tribulation in the first part of His statements in:

> MATTHEW 24
> 29 Immediately after the tribulation of those days shall the sun be darkened, and the moon shall not give her light, and the stars shall fall from heaven, and the powers of the heavens shall be shaken:
> 30 And then shall appear the sign of the Son of man in heaven: and then shall all the tribes of the earth mourn,

and they shall see the Son of man coming in the clouds of heaven with power and great glory.
31 And he shall send his angels with a great sound of a trumpet, and they shall gather together his elect from the four winds, from one end of heaven to the other.

MARK 13
24 But in those days, after that tribulation, the sun shall be darkened, and the moon shall not give her light,

So, the Tribulation ends! But, the story continues—a period of Wrath described in the following portions of the above quotations and in Luke 21 :22–26. The apostle John wrote of similar events in Revelation:

Compare:

Matthew 24:29
to
Revelation 6:12–14 (excerpted)

Immediately after the tribulation of those days
and I beheld when he had opened the sixth seal,

shall the sun be darkened, and
and the sun became black as sackcloth

the moon shall not give her light, and
the moon became as blood;

the stars shall fall from heaven, and
the stars of heaven fell unto the earth,

the powers of the heavens shall be shaken:
and the heaven departed as a scroll . . .

Compare:

Luke 21:22–26 (excerpted)
to
Revelation 6:14–17 (excerpted)

these be the days of vengeance . . . there shall be great distress in the land, and wrath upon this people . . . men's hearts failing them for fear . . . for powers of heaven shall be shaken.

and Signs . . . great men . . . every bondsman . . . said . . . hide us . . . from the wrath of the Lamb: For the great day of his wrath is come: and who shall be able to stand?

Some Conclusions

- *Tribulation* and *Wrath* have different descriptions, events, and periods in time.
- *Tribulation* and *Wrath* should not be considered the same and should not be included into one "Seven-Year Tribulation".

It should be noted that Wrath is mentioned in the Sixth Seal but doesn't actually occur until after the Seventh Seal and Seventh Trumpet. Have heart, this is explained later. The issue here is that *Tribulation* and *Wrath* are not the same activities and do not occur during the same time periods !

10. Believers Experience God's Wrath?

No! No Believer will ever experience the Wrath of God! Previous discussions indicated Scripture evidence that the first resurrection and the Rapture will occur with the last trumpet at 2595 days after covenant confirmation. The last trumpet also ushers in the Wrath of God. There won't be any Believers left on earth to experience any of God's Wrath. The removal of Believers from earth prior to God's Wrath on earth will be the fulfillment of Scripture. Wrath is for nonbelievers:

JOHN 3
[36] He that believeth on the Son hath everlasting life: and he that believeth not the Son shall not see life; but the wrath of God abideth on him.

ROMANS 1
[18] For the wrath of God is revealed from heaven against all ungodliness and unrighteousness of men, who hold the truth in unrighteousness;

ROMANS 5
[9] Much more then, being now justified by his blood, we shall be saved from wrath through him.

EPHESIANS 5
[6] Let no man deceive you with vain words: for because of these things cometh the wrath of God upon the children of disobedience.

I THESSALONIANS 1
[10] And to wait for his Son from heaven, whom he raised from the dead, *even* Jesus, which delivered us from the wrath to come.

I THESSALONIANS 5
[9] For God hath not appointed us to wrath, but to obtain salvation by our Lord Jesus Christ,

It should be very clear that no Christian (true Believer in the LORD Jesus Christ) will experience the Wrath of GOD.

The Sixth Seal contains descriptions of the Wrath of GOD, and it is often concluded that Wrath starts with the Sixth Seal being opened. Actually, the Sixth Seal is a summary of what is to follow later and does not result in GOD's Wrath prior to opening the Seventh Seal and sounding of the first Six Trumpets. (Scripture has many instances where a summary is given first and details are provided later. For example, most of Gen. 2:6–25 provides more detail about the creation of Adam and Eve in Gen. 1:26–29.)

The Sixth Seal itself contains several examples showing it to be a summary of the following events, namely, the "sun darkened, heavens rolled as a scroll and every mountain and island moved". The sun becoming darkened is mentioned in the Sixth Seal and then occurs in the Fifth Trumpet:

REVELATION 6
12 And I beheld when he had opened the sixth seal, and, lo, there was a great earthquake; and the sun became black as sackcloth of hair, and the moon became as blood;

REVELATION 9
1 And the fifth angel sounded, and I saw a star fall from heaven unto the earth: and to him was given the key of the bottomless pit.
2 And he opened the bottomless pit; and there arose a smoke out of the pit, as the smoke of a great furnace; and the sun and the air were darkened by reason of the smoke of the pit.

The Wrath of GOD—Wrath of the Lamb—includes the "mountains and islands moving" due to the "last plague poured from the last vial". This is described in the Sixth Seal (Rev. 6) as an event which actually occurs later (Rev. 16):

REVELATION 6
14 And the heaven departed as a scroll when it is rolled together; and every mountain and island were moved out of their places.

REVELATION 16
20 And every island fled away, and the mountains were not found.

The Sixth Seal prediction of the "heaven departed as a scroll" does not occur until a thousand years later and just prior to the great white throne judgment:

REVELATION 20
11 And I saw a great white throne, and him that sat on it,

from whose face the earth and heaven fled away; and there was found no place for them.
12 And I saw the dead, small and great, stand before God; and the books were opened: and another book was opened, which is *the book* of life: and the dead were judged out of those things which were written in the books, according to their works.

The major factor to consider in evaluating the Sixth Seal is that some of the events could occur again. For instance, the sun could become black more than one time and so could the moon become as blood. But "islands fleeing, mountains not found and heaven departed" are not very likely to happen more than once without some indication in Scripture that they had been restored between events.

Therefore, the Wrath of God is not started with the Sixth Seal. The Wrath activities come later.

Now, returning to the definitions of *vengeance* and *Wrath*, further descriptions are included in the event commonly known as Armageddon:

Isaiah 63
2 Wherefore *art thou* red in thine apparel, and thy garments like him that treadeth in the winevat?
3 I have trodden the winepress alone; and of the people *there was* none with me: for I will tread them in mine anger, and trample them in my fury; and their blood shall be sprinkled upon my garments, and I will stain all my raiment.
4 For the day of vengeance *is* in mine heart, and the year of my redeemed is come.

Revelation 19
13 And he *was* clothed with a vesture dipped in blood: and his name is called The Word of God.
14 And the armies *which were* in heaven followed him upon white horses, clothed in fine linen, white and clean.

> [15] And out of his mouth goeth a sharp sword, that with it he should smite the nations: and he shall rule them with a rod of iron: and he treadeth the winepress of the fierceness and wrath of Almighty God.
> [16] And he hath on *his* vesture and on his thigh a name written, KING OF KINGS, and LORD of LORDS.

GOD's Wrath will occur when the "seventh angel sounded and thy Wrath is come":

> REVELATION 11
> [15] And the seventh angel sounded; and there were great voices in heaven, saying, The kingdoms of this world are become *the kingdoms* of our Lord, and of his Christ; and he shall reign for ever and ever.
> [18] And the nations were angry, and thy wrath is come, and the time of the dead, that they should be judged, and that thou shouldest give reward unto thy servants the prophets and to the saints, and them that fear thy name, small and great; and shouldest destroy them which destroy the earth.

The dead ("should be judged . . . give reward unto thy servants, . . . prophets, . . . saints, and them that fear thy name") is further evidence of resurrection and Rapture. The *dead* refers to the first death, a physical death. It is after resurrection from the first death and the Rapture when GOD's people are judged and given rewards. This will be in heaven during the period of Wrath on earth.

The Seventh Trumpet also relates GOD's Wrath with "drinks of the wine of the Wrath of GOD and great winepress of the Wrath of GOD":

> REVELATION 14
> [10] The same shall drink of the wine of the wrath of God, which is poured out without mixture into the cup of his indignation; and he shall be tormented with fire and brimstone in the presence of the holy angels, and in the presence of the Lamb:
> [19] And the angel thrust in his sickle into the earth, and

gathered the vine of the earth, and cast *it* into the great winepress of the wrath of God.

GOD's Wrath starts when the seventh angel sounds, and then future events lead to torment with fire and brimstone at the final judgment:

REVELATION 14
[11] And the smoke of their torment ascendeth up for ever and ever: and they have no rest day nor night, who worship the beast and his image, and whosoever receiveth the mark of his name.

The Seventh Trumpet ushers in the seven last plagues and the seven golden "vials full of the Wrath of GOD". Since the vials are full, previous events could not include GOD's Wrath:

REVELATION 15
[1] And I saw another sign in heaven, great and marvellous, seven angels having the seven last plagues; for in them is filled up the wrath of God.
[7] And one of the four beasts gave unto the seven angels seven golden vials full of the wrath of God, who liveth for ever and ever.

REVELATION 16
[1] And I heard a great voice out of the temple saying to the seven angels, Go your ways, and pour out the vials of the wrath of God upon the earth.

The last trumpet includes the Wrath of GOD, and its start is when the first resurrection and Rapture occur:

MATTHEW 24
[31] And he shall send his angels with a great sound of a trumpet, and they shall gather together his elect from the four winds, from one end of heaven to the other.

I CORINTHIANS 15
[52] In a moment, in the twinkling of an eye, at the last trump:

for the trumpet shall sound, and the dead shall be raised incorruptible, and we shall be changed.

I THESSALONIANS 4
16 For the Lord himself shall descend from heaven with a shout, with the voice of the archangel, and with the trump of God: and the dead in Christ shall rise first:

Conclusions

- *Resurrection* and *Rapture* occur immediately prior to the release of GOD's Wrath.
- Start of GOD's Wrath can be identified at or shortly after the resurrection-Rapture timing of 2595 days after confirmation of the covenant.

It would seem to be apparent that resurrection, Rapture and GOD's Wrath occur with the Seventh Trumpet. These do not occur all at once. The Seventh Trumpet includes the Seven Plagues, and something happens (finished mystery) when the Seventh Angel "shall begin to sound"—the resurrection and Rapture:

REVELATION 10
7 But in the days of the voice of the seventh angel, when he shall begin to sound, the mystery of God should be finished, as he hath declared to his servants the prophets.

This mystery of GOD is expected to be the resurrection and Rapture:

I CORINTHIANS 15
51 Behold, I show you a mystery; We shall not all sleep, but we shall all be changed,
52 In a moment, in a the twinkling of an eye, at the last trump: for the trumpet shall sound, and the dead shall be raised incorruptible, and we shall be changed.

When the seventh angel shall **begin** to sound, the mystery of GOD is finished and this mystery is defined as "be changed and dead raised": the Rapture! The details of this mystery should be compared to the details given in:

> 1 THESSALONIANS 4
> 16 For the Lord himself shall descend from heaven with a shout, with the voice of the archangel, with the trump of God: and the dead in Christ shall rise first:
> 17 Then we which are alive *and* remain shall be caught up together with them in the clouds, to meet the Lord in the air: and so shall we ever be with the Lord.

Some interpretations indicate the "trump of GOD" in I Thessalonians is not the "last trump" as given in I Corinthians. These trumps supposedly could represent different Raptures, where one trump, the trump of GOD, must be blown by GOD Himself. However, looking at the details of these descriptions shows that they are the same Rapture. For instance, GOD doesn't blow the trump. The only verb is *descend*. The *shout*, *voice* and *trump* are nouns that accompany the Lord.

CHART #9

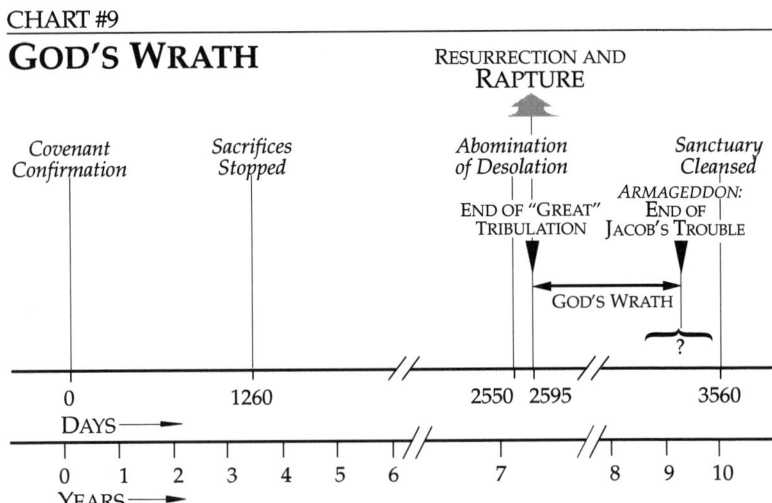

In both descriptions, the "dead are raised". Also, "we [those which are alive] are changed" and must be changed in order to "be caught up together" with the resurrected and changed (incorruptible) dead. Since all the main subject matter is the same in these two descriptions, they must represent the same event: the same trump and the same Rapture.

It seems almost too obvious to mention, but the Great Tribulation ends with resurrection and Rapture. This will not be the same as the end of Jacob's Trouble—it ends at Armageddon. Time periods for Believers and for nonbelieving Israel are different—different programs in God's plan represented by Tribulation and by Jacob's Trouble.

Nonbelieving Israel will experience God's Wrath. Believers will not experience God's Wrath!

11. Believers Experience Tribulation?

Yes! Believers do experience Tribulation:

James 1
2 My brethren, count it all joy when ye fall into divers temptations;
3 Knowing *this,* that the trying of your faith worketh patience.
4 But let patience have *her* perfect work, that ye may be perfect and entire, wanting nothing.

I Peter 2
4 To whom coming, *as unto* a living stone, disallowed indeed of men, but chosen of God, *and* precious,
5 Ye also, as lively stones, are built up a spiritual house, an holy priesthood, to offer up spiritual sacrifices, acceptable to God by Jesus Christ.

In general, trials, testing, tribulation, perseverance, enduring, suffering and patience are used to put Believers under pressure to make precious, living stones for God. Believers can expect some trouble in their lives:

John 16
33 These things I have spoken unto you, that in me ye might have peace. In the world ye shall have tribulation: but be of good cheer; I have overcome the world.

Acts 14
22 Confirming the souls of the disciples, *and* exhorting them to continue in the faith, and that we must through much tribulation enter into the kingdom of God.

Romans 12
21 Be not overcome of evil, but overcome evil with good.

Throughout history, many Believers have had troubles, tribulations, trials and persecutions. This is evident even today when Believers are put to death in many countries.

There is a general relationship with Tribulation and the Coming of Lord Jesus Christ:

I Peter 1
5 Who are kept by the power of God through faith unto salvation ready to be revealed in the last time.
6 Wherein ye greatly rejoice, though now for a season, if need be, ye are in heaviness through manifold temptations:
7 That the trial of your faith, being much more precious than of gold that perisheth, though it be tried with fire, might be found unto praise and honour and glory at the appearing of Jesus Christ:

I Peter 4
12 Beloved, think it not strange concerning the fiery trial which is to try you, as though some strange thing happened unto you:
13 But rejoice, inasmuch as ye are partakers of Christ's sufferings; that, when his glory shall be revealed, ye may be glad also with exceeding joy.

Deuteronomy 4
30 When thou art in tribulation, and all these things are

> come upon thee, *even* in the latter days, if thou turn to the
> LORD thy God, and shalt be obedient unto his voice;
> 31 (For the LORD thy God *is* a merciful God;) he will not
> forsake thee, neither destroy thee, nor forget the covenant
> of thy fathers which he sware unto them.

More specifically, tribulation is part of the end-time events. Therefore, it is called the Tribulation—usually believed to be a seven-year period. In the Olivet Discourse, which deals with the Coming of Jesus Christ and associated end-time events, Jesus Christ said:

> MATTHEW 24
> 9 Then shall they deliver you up to be afflicted, and shall
> kill you: and ye shall be hated of all nations for my name's
> sake.
> 10 And then shall many be offended, and shall betray one
> another, and shall hate one another.

> MARK 13
> 9 But take heed to yourselves: for they shall deliver you up
> to councils; and in the synagogues ye shall be beaten: and
> ye shall be brought before rulers and kings for my sake,
> for a testimony against them.
> 12 Now the brother shall betray the brother to death, and
> the father the son; and children shall rise up against *their*
> parents, and shall cause them to be put to death.
> 13 And ye shall be hated of all *men* for my name's sake: but
> he that shall endure unto the end, the same shall be saved.

> LUKE 21
> 12 But before all these, they shall lay their hands on you, and
> persecute *you*, delivering *you* up to the synagogues, and
> into prisons, being brought before kings and rulers for my
> name's sake.
> 16 And ye shall be betrayed both by parents, and brethren,
> and kinsfolks, and friends; and *some* of you shall they cause
> to be put to death.
> 17 And ye shall be hated of all *men* for my name's sake.

A point could be raised that the Olivet Discourse does not apply to Believers, because it is meant for Jews alone (and the assumption that the Rapture had previously occurred). However, in these recordings of Jesus Christ's own words, the term "for my name's sake" appears four times and "for my sake" is stated once. These words must be directed to Believers of Jesus Christ, not specifically to Jews. In addition, Jesus Christ made a statement that His words were all-inclusive and not directed to Jews only:

MARK 13
37 And what I say unto you I say unto all, Watch.

In the Olivet Discourse, Lord Jesus Christ admonished all to watch for when He comes. The directive *to watch* is stated six times in the three recordings of the Discourse and probably used five times in His oral delivery (Matt. 24:42; 25:13; Mark 13:33, 35, 37; Luke 21:36). Evidently, Lord Jesus Christ meant *watch!* And in the context of the narration in the Discourse, the watching is about His Coming and the gathering of His elect, which is after the Tribulation.

Previously, it was discussed how Scripture places the Rapture before GOD's Wrath. Here, He has shown the Rapture to be after Tribulation. Lord Jesus Christ's instructions to watch for His Coming would seem to negate any idea of a sudden or secret Rapture prior to the Tribulation period.

During the Tribulation, there will be a great deal of persecution of Believers (Saints). Some reference examples have been given, but here are some more:

DANIEL 7
21 I beheld, and the same horn made war with the saints, and prevailed against them;
25 And he shall speak *great* words against the most High, and shall wear out the saints of the most High, and think to change times and laws: and they shall be given into his hand until a time and times and the dividing of time.

Daniel 11
32 And such as do wickedly against the covenant shall he
corrupt by flatteries: but the people that do know their God
shall be strong, and do *exploits*.
33 And they that understand among the people shall instruct
many: yet they shall fall by the sword, and by flame, by
captivity, and by spoil, *many* days.
34 Now when they shall fall, they shall be holpen with a little
help: but many shall cleave to them with flatteries.
35 And *some* of them of understanding shall fall, to try them,
and to purge, and to make *them* white, *even* to the time of
the end: because *it is* yet for a time appointed.

Revelation 13
9 If any man have an ear, let him hear.
10 He that leadeth into captivity shall go into captivity: he
that killeth with the sword must be killed with the sword.
Here is the patience and the faith of the saints.

(See also: Dan. 8:24, 12:10; Rev. 13:7, 14:13.)

The Great Tribulation ends at the resurrection and Rapture, which is just prior to the beginning of God's Wrath. The Great Tribulation is identified by Lord Jesus Christ as starting when the "abomination or desolation stands in the holy place" and when those "in Judea flee":

Matthew 24
15 When ye therefore shall see the abomination of
desolation, spoken of by Daniel the prophet, stand in the
holy place, (whoso readeth, let him understand,)
16 Then let them which be in Judaea flee into the mountains:
21 For then shall be great tribulation, such as was not since
the beginning of the world to this time, no, nor ever shall
be.

Lord Jesus Christ also indicated Israel would be subjected to this great distress as well as to Wrath:

LUKE 21
21 Then let them which are in Judaea flee to the mountains; and let them which are in the midst of it depart out; and let not them that are in the countries enter thereinto.
23 But woe unto them that are with child, and to them that give suck, in those days! for there shall be great distress in the land, and wrath upon this people.

CHART #10

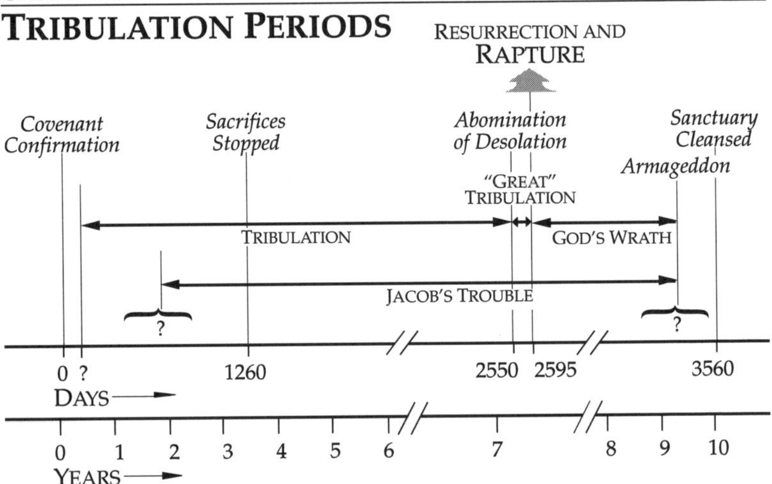

Believers Will Experience Tribulation!

The idea of experiencing any, or all, of the *Tribulation* can be a shock to Believers. Why would Believers be put through this? Believers (true Christians) have *failed*! Christians have failed in obeying GOD's instructions:

MATTHEW 28
20 Teaching them to observe all things whatsoever I have commanded you: and, lo, I am with you always, *even* unto the end of the world. Amen.

MARK 16
15 And he said unto them, Go ye into all the world, and preach the gospel to every creature.

Luke 24
[47] And that repentance and remission of sins should be preached in his name among all nations, beginning at Jerusalem.

There are many who have worked hard and long to accomplish this *Great Commission,* but there have not been enough of them, and few Believers even preach or teach the gospel to family, friends or neighbors. (This writer is far from innocent!) It is so easy to look at the history of Israel and wonder at how they could have possibly strayed from God and disobeyed Him. God knew that it would happen, just as He has known His Church would also do the same.

Adam and Eve disobeyed. Israel disobeyed. His Church has disobeyed. Disobeying is punishable by death—at least the *first* death. The first death is physical. The second death is into the Lake of Fire—the differences to be discussed later.

Romans 6
[23] For the wages of sin is death; but the gift of God *is* eternal life through Jesus Christ our Lord.

Revelation 20
[14] And death and hell were cast into the lake of fire. This is the second death.

Also to be discussed later is when the end-times Tribulation will begin for Believers. This is determined after the unidentified times (question marks on the charts) have been replaced with definitive numbers.

12. How Many Resurrections and Raptures?

It seems that Scripture describes two resurrections and only one Rapture. The first resurrection is for Believers of all previous ages, occurring just prior to the Rapture. The second resurrection is of all nonbelievers and their damnation to hell.

If there were a resurrection and Rapture prior to Tribulation, then at least one more resurrection and Rapture would be required. These additional events would be needed because Revelation is very clear that Believers come out of the Great Tribulation.

Revelation 7
9 After this I beheld, and, lo, a great multitude, which no man could number, of all nations, and kindreds, and people, and tongues, stood before the throne, and before the Lamb, clothed with white robes, and palms in their hands;
14 And I said unto him, Sir, thou knowest. And he said to me, These are they which came out of great tribulation, and have washed their robes, and made them white in the blood of the Lamb.

Revelation 14
15 And another angel came out of the temple, crying with a loud voice to him that sat on the cloud, Thrust in thy sickle, and reap; for the time is come for thee to reap; for the harvest of the earth is ripe.
16 And he that sat on the cloud thrust in his sickle on the earth; and the earth was reaped.

Revelation 15
2 And I saw as it were a sea of glass mingled with fire: and them that had gotten the victory over the beast, and over his image, and over his mark, *and* over the number of his name, stand on the sea of glass, having the harps of God.

Revelation 18
4 And I heard another voice from heaven, saying, Come out of her, my people, that ye be not partakers of her sins, and that ye receive not of her plagues.

In addition, the Olivet Discourse describes a gathering of the elect (Believers) after a Tribulation:

Matthew 24
29 Immediately after the tribulation of those days shall the sun be darkened, and the moon shall not give her light,

and the stars shall fall from heaven, and the powers of the
heavens shall be shaken:
31 And he shall send his angels with a great sound of a
trumpet, and they shall gather together his elect from the
four winds, from one end of heaven to the other.

MARK 13
24 But in those days, after that tribulation, the sun shall be
darkened, and the moon shall not give her light,
27 And then shall he send his angels, and shall gather
together his elect from the four winds, from the uttermost
part of the earth to the uttermost part of heaven.

LUKE 21
25 And there shall be signs in the sun, and in the moon, and
in the stars; and upon the earth distress of nations, with
perplexity; the sea and the waves roaring;
28 And when these things begin to come to pass, then look
up, and lift up your heads; for your redemption draweth
nigh.

These references to a Rapture, or gathering, could be separate events or different descriptions of one. In any case, it is fairly clear that they refer to Believers (overcomers) coming out of the Great Tribulation. Indeed, if there were a pre-Tribulation Rapture, then additional resurrections and Raptures would be described.

It has been shown that Daniel will be resurrected at the time of the Rapture, and he has to wait until 2595 days after covenant confirmation, not before the Tribulation. Other Scripture identify only two resurrections: one resurrection is immediately prior to the *Rapture* (or essentially at the same time), and the other is after the 1000-year reign of Lord Jesus Christ on earth.

The first resurrection is of those whose names are in the Book of Life (Believers). The second resurrection is of those not listed in the Book of Life (nonbelievers), who are condemned to a second death, which is in the Lake of Fire (hell):

REVELATION 20
[15] And whosoever was not found written in the book of life was cast into the lake of fire.

REVELATION 21
[8] But the fearful, and unbelieving, and the abominable, and murderers, and whoremongers, and sorcerers, and idolaters, and all liars, shall have their part in the lake which burneth with fire and brimstone: which is the second death.

In the Gospel of John, we find specific references to "the resurrection of life" and to "the resurrection of damnation". This indicates two resurrections:

JOHN 5
[28] Marvel not at this: for the hour is coming, in the which all that are in the graves shall hear his voice,
[29] And shall come forth; they that have done good, unto the resurrection of life; and they that have done evil, unto the resurrection of damnation.

Additional references imply two resurrections with terms such as *both, just/unjust, they lived/rest of dead, first resurrection* and *second death:*

ACTS 24
[15] And have hope toward God, which they themselves also allow, that there shall be a resurrection of the dead, both of the just and unjust.

REVELATION 20
[4] And I saw thrones, and they sat upon them, and judgment was given unto them: and *I saw* the souls of them that were beheaded for the witness of Jesus, and for the word of God, and which had not worshipped the beast, neither his image, neither had received *his* mark upon their foreheads, or in their hands; and they lived and reigned with Christ a thousand years.
[5] But the rest of the dead lived not again until the thousand

years were finished. This *is* the first resurrection.
[6] Blessed and holy *is* he that hath part in the first resurrection: on such the second death hath no power, but they shall be priests of God and of Christ, and shall reign with him a thousand years.

The above Scripture presents only two resurrections. The first resurrection is at the Coming of Jesus Christ for those who belong to Him:

I CORINTHIANS 15
[20] But now is Christ risen from the dead, *and* become the firstfruits of them that slept.
[21] For since by man *came* death, by man *came* also the resurrection of the dead.
[22] For as in Adam all die, even so in Christ shall all be made alive.
[23] But every man in his own order: Christ the firstfruits; afterward they that are Christ's at his coming.

In Isaiah chapter 26 the last portion vividly describes the plight of Israel during Jacob's Trouble and refers to a resurrection during that time:

ISAIAH 26
[19] Thy dead *men* shall live, *together with* my dead body shall they arise. Awake and sing, ye that dwell in dust: for thy dew *is as* the dew of herbs, and the earth shall cast out the dead.

Isaiah also indicated the people should hide until Tribulation (indignation) should pass over (overpast). Then GOD's Wrath would come in order to "punish the inhabitants of the earth":

ISAIAH 26
[20] Come, my people, enter thou into thy chambers, and shut thy doors about thee: hide thyself as it were for a little moment, until the indignation be overpast.
[21] For, behold, the LORD cometh out of his place to punish

> the inhabitants of the earth for their iniquity: the earth also shall disclose her blood, and shall no more cover her slain.

Isaiah said the resurrection (including himself) would occur while Israel was hiding (probably in the wilderness) and prior to the Wrath of God! This first resurrection is accompanied by the Rapture:

> I Corinthians 15
> 51 Behold, I shew you a mystery; We shall not all sleep, but we shall all be changed,
> 52 In a moment, in the twinkling of an eye, at the last trump: for the trumpet shall sound, and the dead shall be raised incorruptible, and we shall be changed.

> I Thessalonians 4
> 14 For if we believe that Jesus died and rose again, even so them also which sleep in Jesus will God bring with him.
> 15 For this we say unto you by the word of the Lord, that we which are alive *and* remain unto the coming of the Lord shall not prevent them which are asleep.
> 16 For the Lord himself shall descend from heaven with a shout, with the voice of the archangel, and with the trump of God: and the dead in Christ shall rise first:

The first resurrection and *Raptur*e are also given in Daniel, and the second resurrection is identified (implied) as "some to shame and everlasting contempt":

> Daniel 12
> 1 And at that time shall Michael stand up, the great prince which standeth for the children of thy people: and there shall be a time of trouble, such as never was since there was a nation *even* to that same time: and at that time thy people shall be delivered, every one that shall be found written in the book.
> 2 And many of them that sleep in the dust of the earth shall awake, some to everlasting life, and some to shame *and* everlasting contempt.

It would be difficult to interpret the events any different than:

- A first resurrection of all dead Believers (Saints)
- A Rapture of all resurrected and alive Believers (Saints) immediately after the first resurrection
- A second resurrection of nonbelievers at the end of Jesus Christ's reign of one thousand years on earth
- **No second Rapture and no more than two resurrections have been foretold**

A concept of a pre-Tribulation Rapture requires more than one Rapture and more than one resurrection of Believers. These events do not appear to be in Scripture. A concept also exists whereby the first resurrection and the Rapture occur in stages: i.e., not at one time, but in intervals until the total is accumulated. If this were the case, it would seem Scripture would have so stated or have recorded examples to substantiate it.

The various descriptions of resurrected and Raptured individuals in Revelation would need to be of the first resurrection and the Rapture, as told to Daniel.

One rapture! Two resurrections!

13. Alive and Remain

Although parts of specific Scripture passages have been used several times, they are again quoted:

I THESSALONIANS 4
15 For this we say unto you by the word of the Lord, that we which are alive *and* remain unto the coming of the Lord shall not prevent them which are asleep.
17 Then we which are alive *and* remain shall be caught up together with them in the clouds, to meet the Lord in the air: and so shall we ever be with the Lord.

The phrase *alive and remain,* used twice, indicates all living Believers at the time of the Rapture will be Raptured. Being alive is easy to understand, but the "and remain" provides a clue to conditions prevalent at the time of Rapture. The *remain* strongly implies survivors. This would lead into the thought that there may not be many alive at the time of the Rapture—a situation expected if the Rapture were at the end of Great Tribulation.

The Scripture word translated as *remain* is used only in the above verses with a fuller meaning of "to be left all around, to leave all around, to leave over, i.e. to survive".[6,7,8] If there were to be a Rapture prior to any Tribulation, the *alive* would not need modification with *and remain:* i.e., "left all around" in various places because there are few who are alive. The pre-Tribulation Rapture scenario whereby many live Believers are Raptured appears difficult to match the thought of a relatively few left around at the Rapture.

14. Olivet Discourse Prophecies Fulfilled?

Some interpretations of Scripture indicate the Olivet Discourse prophecies have been fulfilled. However, analysis shows only parts of the Discourse prophecies have been fulfilled by historical events and the remainders are yet to occur.

One or two days before His Crucifixion, the Lord Jesus Christ answered some questions about "the end of the world" (Matt. 24:1–3). His answers, usually called the Olivet Discourse, are recorded in Matthew 24–25, Mark 13, and Luke 21.

Interpretations of the Olivet Discourse are varied. The variations include the idea of complete fulfillment in A.D. 70 with the destruction of Jerusalem by the Romans at that time, partial fulfillment in A.D. 70 or no fulfillment as yet having occurred. These interpretations may be based on all of the Discourse recordings; on only one recording, such as in Matthew; or may also include a conclusion that the Revelation prophecies were also fulfilled in A.D. 70.

The premise presented here is that the Discourse actually describes two different destructions of Jerusalem, rather than only one event, which has been the usual assumption. Luke recorded prophecies describing the historical event of A.D. 70 and followed with prophecies about the second (future) event. Matthew and Mark only recorded prophecies about the second event.

That there are two different events described is shown because the prophecies contain different beginning conditions, different purposes, different groups of people, different results and different timing references.

Notice that Luke 21:23 describes events involving "this people":

> LUKE 21
> 23 But woe unto them that are with child, and to them that give suck, in those days! for there shall be great distress in the land, and wrath upon this people.

In contrast, Matthew 24:14 refers to "all the world" and "all nations". Matthew 24:21, 30, 31; Mark 13:10, 13, 26–27 make additional references to *world, they, four winds, one end of heaven to the other, all nations, all men, elect from uttermost part of the earth to the uttermost part of heaven:*

> MATTHEW 24
> 14 And this gospel of the kingdom shall be preached in all the world for a witness unto all nations; and then shall the end come.

Luke wrote about *this people* who are those specifically of Jerusalem and Judea (Luke 21:20–21), which refers to Jews. Matthew and Mark identify *all the world, all nations, and men,* etc., indicating different groups of people are involved. Luke describes the historical A.D. 70 event, which was directed to Jews, and Matthew and Mark present an event involving *all the world, nations and men*: an event not yet having occurred.

Luke precedes his description of *these people* by identifying Jerusalem compassed with armies:

LUKE 21
[20] And when ye shall see Jerusalem compassed with armies, then know that the desolation thereof is nigh.

Matthew/Mark describe an event that will start with "see the abomination of desolation" (Matt. 24:15; Mark 13:14):

MATTHEW 24
[15] When ye therefore shall see the abomination of desolation, spoken of by Daniel the prophet, stand in the holy place, (whoso readeth, let him understand,)

"Jerusalem compassed with armies" and "see the abomination of desolation" could be the beginning of the same event, but the Scripture does not so state. This difference in beginning conditions reinforces, but does not prove, the premise of two different events for two different groups (i.e., one event for Jews and one for all nations).

Luke indicated that there would be "wrath upon this people" and had also stated there would be "vengeance and distress":

LUKE 21
[22] For these be the days of vengeance, that all things which are written may be fulfilled.
[23] But woe unto them that are with child, and to them that give suck, in those days! for there shall be great distress in the land, and wrath upon this people.

Wrath, vengeance, and *distress* have similar meanings, whereby anger is carried out for punishment. This is different than the *tribulation* associated with the second event: *tribulation* and *affliction* are pressure or a trial to test endurance and patience.

MATTHEW 24
[21] For than shall be great tribulation, such as was not since

the beginning of the world to this time, no, nor ever shall be.

MARK 13
[19] For *in* those days shall be affliction, such as was not from the beginning of the creation which God created unto this time, neither shall be.

The A.D. 70 destruction of Jerusalem was to punish the Jews, and the second/future event will be to try and test followers of Jesus Christ:

REVELATION 14
[12] Here is the patience of the saints: here *are* they that keep the commandments of God, and the faith of Jesus.
[13] And I heard a voice from heaven saying unto me, Write, Blessed *are* the dead which die in the Lord from henceforth: Yea, saith the Spirit, that they may rest from their labours; and their works do follow them.

Luke recorded that the "wrath upon this people" (the Jews) would include "they shall be led away captive unto all nations". This is precisely what happened after A.D.70! The dispersion of Jews throughout the world, along with the destruction of Jerusalem, are history!

Also, "Jerusalem shall be trodden down of the Gentiles, until the times of the Gentiles be fulfilled":

LUKE 21
[24] And they shall fall by the edge of the sword, and shall be led away captive into all nations: and Jerusalem shall be trodden down of the Gentiles, until the times of the Gentiles be fulfilled.

Jerusalem has been trodden down of the Gentiles for over nineteen hundred years since the first event and will continue "until the times of the Gentiles be fulfilled". There will be a second event when "the times of the Gentiles be fulfilled".

The second event is going to happen! Luke continued to write that after "the times of the Gentiles be fulfilled":

LUKE 21
25 And there shall be signs in the sun, and in the moon, and in the stars; and upon the earth distress of nations, with perplexity; the sea and the waves roaring;
26 Men's hearts failing them for fear, and for looking after those things which are coming on the earth: for the powers of heaven shall be shaken.
27 And then shall they see the Son of man coming in a cloud with power and great glory.
29 And he spake to them a parable; Behold the fig tree, and all the trees;

These are the same basic descriptions that Matthew and Mark gave in their records of the events involving "all the world, nation, and men" (Matt. 24:29–31; Mark 13:24–27), where all three records describe activities relating to *signs, sun, moon, stars, powers of heaven shaken* and *see the Son of man coming.*

The "times of the Gentiles be fulfilled" will be immediately after the Tribulation, as described in Mark 13:24 and:

MATTHEW 24
29 Immediately after the tribulation of those days shall the sun be darkened, and the moon shall not give her light, and the stars shall fall from heaven, and the powers of the heavens shall be shaken:
30 And then shall appear the sign of the Son of man in heaven: and then shall all the tribes of the earth mourn, and they shall see the Son of man coming in the clouds of heaven with power and great glory.
31 And he shall send his angels with a great sound of a trumpet, and they shall gather together his elect from the four winds, from one end of heaven to the other.
32 Now learn a parable of the fig tree; When his branch is yet tender, and putteth forth leaves, ye know that summer is nigh:

And, "then . . . the Son of man coming . . . gather together his elect" (Amen!). So, Luke had recorded the first event about the destruction of Jerusalem in A.D. 70 and then also recorded the final stages of the second event complementing the descriptions given by Matthew and Mark. Since Matthew and Mark recorded activities that involve the "world and all tribes of the earth", they will correspond to the Revelation descriptions of *every eye, they that dwell upon the earth, all kindreds, and tongues, and nations:*

> REVELATION 1
> 7 Behold, he cometh with clouds; and every eye shall see him, and they *also* which pierced him: and all kindreds of the earth shall wail because of him. Even so, A-men.

The Second Advent has not yet occurred, Christ has not been seen (physically) and the prophecies in Revelation have not been fulfilled!

The previous statement of "every eye shall see him" brings up another issue about whether the Olivet Discourse (and some Revelation) prophecies have been fulfilled. Unfortunately, there has been a persuasive argument that the word *see* does not have the literal meaning of *see*: i.e., *see* would not be a physical activity when Jesus Christ "cometh with clouds". The Greek word used for *see* in Revelation 1:7 is also used in Mark 13:26; Luke 21:27, and:

> MATTHEW 24
> 30 And then shall appear the sign of the Son of man in heaven: and then shall all the tribes of the earth mourn, and they shall see the Son of man coming in the clouds of heaven with power and great glory.

> REVELATION 22
> 4 And they shall see his face; and his name shall be in their foreheads.

The idea that the Olivet Discourse prophecies have been fulfilled requires a figurative, perspective, or spiritual interpretation of Scripture, whereby the *see* used in these verses does not mean *see* in a natural or literal way. To see would have to mean perceiving, understanding, or being aware of fulfillment in one's mind. However, the word that is used is the Greek term of *optanomai* or *optomai* (the root for our English word of *opthamology*), and it specifically means to "gaze with wide open eyes".[9]

If Jesus Christ had intended the meaning of *see* to be "perception" or "understanding" in contrast to physical gazing, surely He would have used a suitable Greek term with that specific meaning! In such a case, Jesus Christ could have used the word *eido* when He meant "perceive with the mind, understand, experience, or know intuitively", which could result from physical sight.[10] This is entirely different from "gaze with wide open eyes, behold or witness".

Actually, Jesus Christ did use the term *eido,* which has been translated to *see,* when referring to "this generation" in Discourse statements given in Mark 13:29–30; Luke 21:31–32 and:

> Matthew 24
> [33] So likewise ye, when ye shall see all these things, know that it is near, *even* at the doors.
> [34] Verily I say unto you, This generation shall not pass, till all these things be fulfilled.

So, in the Olivet Discourse, Lord Jesus said the "generation [that] shall see all these things [is] this generation, [which] shall not pass till all these things be fulfilled".

"This generation [will] see [in the sense of perceive, understand, experience, and know] all these things. This [same] generation [also] shall see [gaze with eyes, behold, witness] the Son of man coming in the clouds". Neither of these *see* (perceive nor gaze) activities have yet occurred!

"This generation" of end times in the Olivet Discourse is not "this generation" of *scribes and Pharisees, hypocrites* and *serpents, ye generation of vipers* whom Jesus Christ confronted prior to His Discourse at Olivet:

MATTHEW 23
27 Woe unto you, scribes and Pharisees, hypocrites! for ye are like unto whited sepulchres, which indeed appear beautiful outward, but are within full of dead *men's* bones, and of all uncleanness.
32 Fill ye up then the measure of your fathers.
33 *Ye* serpents, *ye* generation of vipers, how can ye escape the damnation of hell?
35 That upon you may come all the righteous blood shed upon the earth, from the blood of righteous Abel unto the blood of Zacharias son of Barachiah, whom ye slew between the temple and the altar.
36 Verily I say unto you, All these things shall come upon this generation.

This generation of scribes, Pharisees and hypocrites is the "whited sepulchres, ye serpents, ye generation of vipers". They are "this generation upon whom all these things shall come". Here, *these things* refer to "Woe, the measure of your fathers damnation, upon you all the righteous blood shed". They received these things in the destruction of Jerusalem completed in A.D.70.

Jesus Christ identified two distinctly different generations as "this generation". The discussions were at different times, in different places, to different audiences and with different results intended.

The Olivet Discourse prophecies were not totally fulfilled by the A.D.70 destruction of Jerusalem. Jesus Christ identified different generations that would be involved in the two different prophecies. The first destruction of Jerusalem, as prophesied in the Olivet Discourse, resulted in a dispersion of the Jews until "time of the Gentiles be fulfilled":

LUKE 21
24 And they shall fall by the edge of the sword, and shall be

led away captive into all nations: and Jerusalem shall be trodden down of the Gentiles, until the times of the Gentiles be fulfilled.

The second destruction will result in gathering His elect and putting the Jews back upon their land:

MARK 13
27 And then shall he send his angels, and shall gather together his elect from the four winds, from the uttermost part of the earth to the uttermost part of heaven.

AMOS 9
15 And I will plant them upon their land, and they shall no more be pulled up out of their land which I have given them, saith the Lord thy God.

Conclusions

- Luke recorded the Olivet Discourse prophecy of Jerusalem's destruction, which was fulfilled in A.D. 70.
- Luke also recorded the end-times prophecies that corroborate the Olivet Discourse prophecies in Matthew and Mark.
- Greek word meanings cannot be used to conclude any perception nor figurative return of Christ at the A.D. 70 destruction of Jerusalem.
- "This generation" *(ye generation of vipers)* is not "this generation" that will witness when (with gazing eyes) Jesus Christ "cometh with clouds".
- Only a portion of the Olivet Discourse prophecies have been fulfilled by historical events of A.D. 70.
- Most of the Olivet Discourse prophecies, along with the Revelation prophecies, are yet to be fulfilled.

15. Who Is Taken?

On two occasions recorded in Scripture, Jesus Christ made some statements concerning "one shall be taken, and the other left". The statements were when He was answering Pharisees about when the kingdom of God should come (Luke 17:20, 34–36) and during the Olivet Discourse:

> MATTHEW 24
> 40 Then shall two be in the field; the one shall be taken, and
> the other left.
> 41 Two *women shall be* grinding at the mill; the one shall be
> taken, and the other left.

Usually, the "one shall be taken" is thought to be a Believer who is taken up at the Rapture. However, there is another school of thought that holds that those taken are the "tares gathered in the time of harvest":

> MATTHEW 13
> 30 Let both grow together until the harvest: and in the time
> of harvest I will say to the reapers, Gather ye together first
> the tares, and bind them in bundles to burn them: but
> gather the wheat into my barn.

This other school of thought would have nonbelievers being taken from the earth and the Believers left. Are Believers taken or are the tares taken? Who is taken?

Believers are the ones taken! The "tares are gathered to burn". Usage of *taken* cannot refer to the tares. The Greek word in question is used fifty times in the New Testament and is translated as *taken* or *receive,* such as in Jesus Christ's words:

> JOHN 14
> 3 And if I go and prepare a place for you, I will come again,
> and receive you unto myself; that where I am, *there* ye may
> be also.

> LUKE 17
> 34 I tell you, in that night there shall be two *men* in one bed;
> the one shall be taken, and the other shall be left.
> 35 Two *women* shall be grinding together; the one shall be
> taken, and the other left.

> [36] Two *men* shall be in the field; the one shall be taken, and the other left.

In all fifty cases, the one *taken* or *received* benefited, or would benefit (usually in the long term) from the action. Every usage of the Greek word used for *taken* or *receive* is presented in the Appendix along with key excerpts showing the intended usage.

In forty-three uses, the ones taken, taking, receiving, being received are specifically identified as Jesus Christ (Himself), a devout Jew or a Believer. There is no justification for thinking the additional five uses in Jesus Christ's end-time teachings should be any different. The remaining two uses of the word benefited the ones taken, and this is shown in the Appendix.

Conclusions

- Believers are the ones *taken* or *received*, and others are left.
- Those "taken" cannot be the tares, which are "gathered and bound for burning".

16. One Body

If there were a Rapture prior to the Tribulation, there are still going to be Believers in the Tribulation and Great Tribulation who will be resurrected or Raptured. Scripture evidence of Believers being in these end-time periods has been presented previously. The pre-Tribulation Rapture view would have that these Believers are resurrected, or Raptured, in other such events during end times. The involved Believers are thought to be those who are born-again and saved after a first resurrection and the Rapture. A second or even a third resurrection/Rapture would occur prior to Lord Jesus Christ establishing His Kingdom on earth.

Additional resurrections/Raptures would require more than one Body of Christ or require His Body be separated into parts. According to Scripture, there is only one Body of Christ:

EPHESIANS 1
22 And hath put all *things* under his feet, and gave him *to be*
the head over all *things* to the church,
23 Which is his body, the fulness of him that filleth all in all.

EPHESIANS 2
16 And that he might reconcile both unto God in one body
by the cross, having slain the enmity thereby:

EPHESIANS 3
6 That the Gentiles should be fellow heirs, and of the same
body, and partakers of his promise in Christ by the gospel.

EPHESIANS 4
12 For the perfecting of the saints, for the work of the
ministry, for the edifying of the body of Christ:

GALATIANS 3
28 There is neither Jew nor Greek, there is neither bond nor
free, there is neither male nor female: for ye are all one in
Christ Jesus.

ROMANS 12
4 For as we have many members in one body, and all
members have not the same office:
5 So we, *being* many, are one body in Christ, and every one
members one of another.

I CORINTHIANS 12
12 For as the body is one, and hath many members and all
the members of that one body, being many, are one body:
so also *is* Christ.
13 For by one Spirit are we all baptized into one body,
whether *we be* Jews or Gentiles, whether *we be* bond or free;
and have been all made to drink into one Spirit.
18 But now hath God set the members every one of them in
the body, as it hath pleased him.

(See also Eph. 4:15–16; 5:30; I Cor. 12:20, 27; Col. 1:18; 2:17, 19; Heb. 13:3).

There is no indication that the Body of Christ would be separated into parts or groups. Actually, it is not to be divided:

I CORINTHIANS 12
25 That there should be no schism in the body; but *that* the members should have the same care one for another.

The word *schism* means "split, gap or division". Believers (members of the Body) are not to cause splits or divisions within the Body: i.e., within the Church. If Jesus Christ doesn't want His Body to be divided by any member(s), it would seem unlikely He would do so with separate resurrections or Raptures.

The precept of "no schism in the body" is so members have some "care for one another", which would be difficult if some have been taken from the earth, especially "understanding ones".

Daniel indicated experienced, understanding Believers would be on earth when the sacrifices are stopped and until the "abomination that maketh desolate":

DANIEL 11
31 And arms shall stand on his part, and they shall pollute the sanctuary of strength, and shall take away the daily *sacrifice*, and they shall place the abomination that maketh desolate.
32 And such as do wickedly against the covenant shall he corrupt by flatteries: but the people that do know their God shall be strong, and do *exploits*.
33 And they that understand among the people shall instruct many: yet they shall fall by the sword, and by flame, by captivity, and by spoil, *many* days.
35 And *some* of them of understanding shall fall, to try them, and to purge, and to make *them* white, *even* to the time of the end: because *it is* yet for a time appointed.

Actually, the concept that nonbelievers may be converted after a pre-Tribulation Rapture violates GOD's instructions concerning church leadership and teachers. After the Rapture, there will not be anyone taught by sound doctrine who is "not a novice" capable of "rightly dividing the word of truth":

TITUS 1
9 Holding fast the faithful word as he hath been taught, that he may be able by sound doctrine both to exhort and to convince the gainsayers.

I TIMOTHY 3
6 Not a novice, lest being lifted up with pride he fall into the condemnation of the devil.

II TIMOTHY 2
15 Study to shew thyself approved unto God, a workman that needeth not to be ashamed, rightly dividing the word of truth.

The concept of multiple resurrections and Raptures would require separation of parts of His Body and show a partiality to one part over another. This is very difficult to reconcile with Scripture.

The term *hope* is often related to the *resurrection, coming of Christ, Rapture, manifestation and realization of life* (eternal) and *endurance under trial.*[11]

TITUS 2
13 Looking for that blessed hope, and the glorious appearing of the great God and our Saviour Jesus Christ;

EPHESIANS 4
4 *There is* one body, and one Spirit, even as ye are called in one hope of your calling;

ACTS 23
6 But when Paul perceived that the one part were

Sadducees, and the other Pharisees, he cried out in the council, Men *and* brethren, I am a Pharisee, the son of a Pharisee: of the hope and resurrection of the dead I am called in question.

COLOSSIANS 1
27 To whom God would make known what *is* the riches of the glory of this mystery among the Gentiles; which is Christ in you, the hope of glory:

I THESSALONIANS 5
8 But let us, who are of the day, be sober, putting on the breastplate of faith and love; and for an helmet, the hope of salvation.

The "blessed hope" is one hope, hope of resurrection, hope of Rapture, hope of salvation (manifested), hope of calling, etc. The "blessed hope" strongly implies there is only one resurrection and only one Rapture of Believers.

Multiple resurrections and Raptures of Believers don't seem to be supported by Scripture.

17. Carcass (Body) and Eagles

Twice, Lord Jesus Christ made comments about a body (or carcass) and eagles. Both times He was specifically explaining His Coming and the Rapture. Sometime prior to His final entrance into Jerusalem, Jesus Christ gave the disciples a brief overview (Luke 17:20–37) of the Olivet Discourse, which was then delivered in full within days before His Crucifixion. A description of His Coming is followed with a description of the Rapture:

LUKE 17
34 I tell you, in that night there shall be two *men* in one bed; the one shall be taken, and the other shall be left.
35 Two *women* shall be grinding together; the one shall be taken, and the other left.

[36] Two *men* shall be in the field; the one shall be taken, and
the other left.
[37] And they answered and said unto him, Where, Lord?
And he said unto them, Wheresoever the body *is,* thither
will the eagles be gathered together.

These comments were repeated in the Olivet Discourse:

MATTHEW 24
[27] For as the lightning cometh out of the east, and shineth
even unto the west; so shall also the coming of the Son of
man be.
[28] For wheresoever the carcass is, there will the eagles be
gathered together.

Since His Coming and the Rapture are described to be in the times of Tribulation, pre-Tribulation Rapture adherents would indicate this is a second Rapture; dead bodies would be expected during the Tribulation periods, and they would be the last Believers to be resurrected.

However, it should be noted that Jesus Christ's references to the body and the carcass are singular and refer to one body! The same term has been translated to *body* (meaning "dead body") and to *carcass*. This same term is used elsewhere in Scripture only for the dead bodies of John the Baptist, Jesus Christ, and GOD's Two Witnesses:[12]

MATTHEW 14
[10] And he sent, and beheaded John in the prison.
[12] And his disciples came, and took up the body, and buried
it, and went and told Jesus.

MARK 15
[45] And when he knew *it* of the centurion, he gave the body
to Joseph.

MARK 6
[29] And when his disciples heard *of it,* they came and took
up his corpse, and laid it in a tomb.

REVELATION 11
[8] And their dead bodies *shall lie* in the street of the great city, which spiritually is called Sodom and Egypt, where also our Lord was crucified.
[9] And they of the people and kindreds and tongues and nations shall see their dead bodies three days and an half, and shall not suffer their dead bodies to be put in graves.

These Scripture examples, where the word for *body* or *carcass* is used, indicate some commonalties: *killed* (or *fallen*), *filled with the Holy Spirit, sent by GOD, loved by GOD* and *belong to GOD*. The singular *body* is referring to the Believers: the Body of Christ! The eagles are angels who are the ones gathering the elect in the Rapture:

REVELATION 12
[14] And to the woman were given two wings of a great eagle, that she might fly into the wilderness, into her place, where she is nourished for a time, and times, and half a time, from the face of the serpent.

MATTHEW 24
[31] And he shall send his angels with a great sound of a trumpet, and they shall gather together his elect from the four winds, from one end of heaven to the other.

It should be concluded that the angels gather all the fallen Saints and live Believers—one Body—at one time.

18. Parable of the Fig Tree

Immediately after describing the Rapture (and resurrection) in His Olivet Discourse, Jesus Christ tells the parable of the fig tree:

MATTHEW 24
[32] Now learn a parable of the fig tree; When his branch is yet tender, and putteth forth leaves, ye know that summer *is* nigh:

> [33] So likewise ye, when ye shall see all these things, know that it is near , *even* at the doors.
>
> MARK 13
> [28] Now learn a parable of the fig tree; When her branch is yet tender, and putteth forth leaves, ye know that summer is near:
> [29] So ye in like manner, when ye shall see these things come to pass, know that it is nigh, *even* at the doors.
>
> LUKE 21
> [29] And he spake to them a parable; Behold the fig tree, and all the trees;
> [30] When they now shoot forth, ye see and know of your own selves that summer is now nigh at hand.
> [31] So likewise ye, when ye see these things come to pass, know ye that the kingdom of God is nigh at hand.

This parable is generally figured to mean the signs given in the Discourse will indicate the fulfillment of His Coming is to be soon, just as seeing leaves on a tree indicates summer is coming soon. This is a very simple statement meaning what it says! It also may mean that when Israel regains worship and sacrifices, His Coming will be soon.

The parable is recorded three times in Scripture whereas some details of the Discourse are not reiterated as often. Could there be more intended with this parable?

The fig tree is unique in the production of fruit, and Jesus Christ's listeners would have known there are three crops. The first crop of figs buds and grows before the leaves start forming. These figs usually fall to the ground prior to harvest of the second crop. The first figs are the most desirable due to tenderness and taste—also known as the *firstfruits*.

The second crop of figs starts growing after the leaves form and grows under the leaves. (Could this be symbolic of protection by the Holy Spirit?) The second crop is harvested by picking and is considered the *harvest*.

Then the third crop forms. It is poor in texture, color, and taste. It is not harvested; it is left to rot on the tree or is blown away in winter storms.

The parable refers to Jesus Christ's previous statements and was given immediately after His telling about coming to gather the elect:

> MATTHEW 24
> 31 And he shall send his angels with a great sound of a trumpet, and they shall gather together his elect from the four winds, from one end of heaven to the other.

> MARK 13
> 27 And then shall he send his angels, and shall gather together his elect from the four winds, from the uttermost part of the earth to the uttermost part of heaven.

> LUKE 21
> 27 And then shall they see the Son of man coming in a cloud with power and great glory.
> 28 And when these things begin to come to pass, then look up, and lift up your heads; for your redemption draweth nigh.

It appears that the parable was also intended to emphasize the one resurrection and one Rapture of Believers. The first crop would represent those who have died (fallen)—firstfruits—and are resurrected. The second crop would represent those who have been protected until harvest—the Rapture. The third crop is left to rot, symbolizing the second resurrection to damnation.

Multiple resurrections and Raptures of Believers would, again, seem unlikely.

Chapter Four

19. Apostle John Raptured?

The pre-Tribulation Rapture concept indicates that the apostle John was Raptured into heaven during Revelation and is symbolic of Believers. The symbolism shows Believers are to be Raptured prior to the events presented in Revelation:

> REVELATION 4
> 1 After this I looked, and, behold, a door *was* opened in heaven: and the first voice which I heard *was* as it were of a trumpet talking with me; which said, Come up hither, and I will shew thee things which must be hereafter.
> 2 And immediately I was in the Spirit: and, behold, a throne was set in heaven, and *one* sat on the throne.

The trumpet mentioned is supposed to represent the "last trump":

> I CORINTHIANS 15
> 52 In a moment, in the twinkling of an eye, at the last trump: for the trumpet shall sound, and the dead shall be raised incorruptible, and we shall be changed.

This trumpet in Revelation is a description of a voice and doesn't seem to be related to the actual sounding, or blowing, of a trumpet.

John was in the Spirit and did not have a changed nor an incorruptible body:

I CORINTHIANS 15
[53] For this corruptible must put on incorruption, and this mortal *must* put on immortality.

And, John referred to what he saw as a *vision*:

REVELATION 9
[17] And thus I saw the horses in the vision, and them that sat on them, having breastplates of fire, and of jacinth, and brimstone: and the heads of the horses *were* as the heads of lions; and out of their mouths issued fire and smoke and brimstone.

The trumpet was a description of a voice, not a sounding; John was in the Spirit, not in actual presence; and he was seeing a vision, not in actual presence.

Regardless of when the Rapture occurs, the Believers/ Saints will remain in Heaven until the end-time activities are completed. Then they return to earth with Lord Jesus Christ for His reign on earth for one thousand years:

REVELATION 20
[6] Blessed and holy *is* he that hath part in the first resurrection: on such the second death hath no power, but they shall be priests of God and of Christ, and shall reign with him a thousand years.

John (or his spirit) didn't stay in Heaven during much of what he saw. John was:

. . . on earth, watching an angel:

REVELATION 10
[1] And I saw another mighty angel come down from heaven, clothed with a cloud: and a rainbow *was* upon his head, and his face *was* as it were the sun, and his feet as pillars of fire:

. . . on earth, hearing a voice from Heaven:

Revelation 10
[4] And when the seven thunders had uttered their voices, I was about to write: and I heard a voice from heaven saying unto me, Seal up those things which the seven thunders uttered, and write them not.

. . . on earth, taking the book from an angel:

Revelation 10
[8] And the voice which I heard from heaven spake unto me again, and said, Go *and* take the little book which is open in the hand of the angel which standeth upon the sea and upon the earth.

. . . on earth, standing upon the sand:

Revelation 13
[1] And I stood upon the sand of the sea, and saw a beast rise up out of the sea, having seven heads and ten horns, and upon his horns ten crowns, and upon his heads the name of blasphemy.

. . . on earth, carried into the wilderness:

Revelation 17
[3] So he carried me away in the spirit into the wilderness: and I saw a woman sit upon a scarlet-coloured beast, full of names of blasphemy, having seven heads and ten horns.

. . . on earth, watching an angel come down from Heaven:

Revelation 18
[1] And after these things I saw another angel come down from heaven, having great power; and the earth was lightened with his glory.

. . . on earth, watching an angel come down from Heaven:

Revelation 20
[1] And I saw an angel come down from heaven, having the

key of the bottomless pit and a great chain in his hand.

. . . on earth, carried away to a high mountain:

REVELATION 21
10 And he carried me away in the spirit to a great and high mountain, and shewed me that great city, the holy Jerusalem, descending out of heaven from God,

If John is to be considered symbolic of the Believers (Body of Christ) during end times, the conclusion really should be that, like John, the Believers will be on earth during much of the activity described in Revelation.

20. Elders Represent Raptured Church?

The twenty-four elders in Revelation performed functions (or duties) and have knowledge similar to the angels and other supernatural beings in heaven. As in the case of the apostle John, some Rapture viewpoints would have the elders Raptured and representing a Raptured Church. One quotation aptly describes the viewpoint:"These twenty-four elders stand for the total church from Pentecost to the rapture. Therefore, I can say categorically and dogmatically that here is the church in heaven."[13]

The twenty-four elders, beasts and angels are arranged where four beasts are "in the midst of the throne, and around about the throne . . . elders round about the throne . . . angels surrounding the beasts and elders . . ." and they all often join together in worship:

REVELATION 4
6 And before the throne *there was* a sea of glass like unto crystal: and in the midst of the throne, and round about the throne, *were* four beasts full of eyes before and behind.

REVELATION 4
4 And round about the throne *were* four and twenty seats: and upon the seats I saw four and twenty elders sitting,

clothed in white raiment; and they had on their heads crowns of gold.

Revelation 5
[11] And I beheld, and I heard the voice of many angels round about the throne and the beasts, and the elders: and the number of them was ten thousand times ten thousand, and thousands of thousands;
[12] Saying with a loud voice, Worthy is the Lamb that was slain to receive power, and riches, and wisdom, and strength, and honour, and glory, and blessing.

Revelation 7
[11] And all the angels stood round about the throne, and *about* the elders and the four beasts, and fell before the throne on their faces, and worshipped God,
[12] Saying, Amen: Blessing, and glory, and wisdom, and thanksgiving, and honour, and power, and might, *be* unto our God for ever and ever. Amen.

The twenty-four elders are not included with "much people" just prior to their worship after the Rapture. Instead, they were worshipping with the four beasts:

Revelation 19
[1] And after these things I heard a great voice of much people in heaven, saying, Alleluia; Salvation, and glory, and honour, and power, unto the Lord our God:
[4] And the four and twenty elders and the four beasts fell down and worshipped God that sat on the throne, saying, Amen; Alleluia.

If John and the elders were Raptured (supposedly) at the same time, it would not follow that the elders knew what was happening whereas John did not know—they should have had the same understanding:

Revelation 5
[5] And one of the elders saith unto me, Weep not: behold, the Lion of the tribe of Juda, the Root of David, hath

prevailed to open the book, and to loose the seven seals thereof.

REVELATION 7
[13] And one of the elders answered, saying unto me, What are these which are arrayed in white robes? and whence came they?
[14] I said unto him, Sir, Thou knowest. And he said to me, These are they which came out of great tribulation, and have washed their robes, and made them white in the blood of the Lamb.

It is also difficult to comprehend why the apostle John would refer to a fellow Rapturee (elder) as "Sir".

The apostle John was told at the beginning of Revelation that it would be shown to him by an angel, and this was confirmed later in Revelation:

REVELATION 1
[1] The Revelation of Jesus Christ, which God gave unto him, to shew unto his servants things which must shortly come to pass; and he sent and signified *it* by his angel unto his servant John:

REVELATION 22
[8] And I John saw these things, and heard *them*. And when I had heard and seen, I fell down to worship before the feet of the angel which shewed me these things.
[16] I Jesus have sent mine angel to testify unto you these things in the churches. I am the root and the offspring of David, *and* the bright and morning star.

Some of the information John received had been from the elders. The elders must be supernatural beings—evidently of elder rank—otherwise the words of Jesus Christ would have been incorrect. This latter option must be considered with trepidation!

Another view held in support of a pre-Tribulation Rapture relates to a new song containing phrases of "redeemed us . . .

made us . . . kings and priests and we shall reign . . ." This is supposed to indicate the elders are Raptured:

> REVELATION 5
> [8] And when he had taken the book, the four beasts and four *and* twenty elders fell down before the Lamb, having every one of them harps, and golden vials full of odours, which are the prayers of saints.
> [9] And they sung a new song, saying, Thou art worthy to take the book, and to open the seals thereof: for thou wast slain, and hast redeemed us to God by thy blood out of every kindred, and tongue, and people, and nation;
> [10] And hast made us unto our God kings and priests: and we shall reign on the earth.

Later versions of the Bible indicate the words should be changed: i.e., *us* to *men; us* to *them;* and *we* to *they.* If these changes are correct, the song would not show the elders to be Raptured. If the version quoted is correct, then the four beasts must also have been Raptured because they also sang the song. **The four beasts in the midst and round about the throne are not Raptured!**

No matter which translation is used, the "new song" verses can't be made to fit a justification for indicating the elders represent a Raptured Church.

The elders are not Raptured!

21. The Church in Revelation?

After Revelation 3, the word *Church* is not mentioned. This has been interpreted to indicate the Church has been Raptured. The concept has been reinforced with the idea that the apostle John and the twenty-four elders represent the Church in Heaven and will not be on earth during Revelation's end-time activities. If this were so, why even bother reading Revelation? Unfortunately, it has been noticed that this is the attitude of many who believe the Rapture will have occurred before the First Seal is opened.

Yet the Revelation of Jesus Christ is intended to be read, studied, and learned. It is the only book in Scripture where reading is specifically encouraged!

> REVELATION 1
> [3] Blessed *is* he that readeth, and they that hear the words of this prophecy, and keep those things which are written therein: for the time is at hand.
>
> REVELATION 22
> [7] Behold, I come quickly: Blessed *is* he that keepeth the sayings of the prophecy of this book.

Although the term *church* is not used after Chapter Three, it should be noted that each letter to a church angel ends with the admonition like "He that hath an ear, let him hear what the Spirit saith unto the churches; . . ." The letters to the churches are to be applied to all other churches everywhere and to each individual. The admonition is stated seven times! Seven times there is a shift of emphasis from church to the individual!

The Emphasis in Scripture is to Individuals!

> JOHN 3
> [16] For God so loved the world, that he gave his only begotten Son, that whosoever believeth in him should not perish, but have everlasting life.
> [18] He that believeth on him is not condemned: but he that believeth not is condemned already, because he hath not believed in the name of the only begotten Son of God.
>
> JOHN 6
> [40] And this is the will of him that sent me, that every one which seeth the Son, and believeth on him, may have everlasting life: and I will raise him up at the last day.

II PETER 3
[9] The Lord is not slack concerning his promise, as some men count slackness; but is long-suffering to us-ward, not willing that any should perish, but that all should come to repentance.

REVELATION 1
[5] And from Jesus Christ, *who is* the faithful witness, *and* the first begotten of the dead, and the prince of the kings of the earth. Unto him that loved us, and washed us from our sins in his own blood,
[6] And hath made us kings and priests unto God and his Father; to him *be* glory and dominion for ever and ever. Amen.

Lack of the word *church* after Chapter Three in Revelation should not be taken to mean that the Church has been Raptured.

Jesus Christ is most interested in each individual who belongs to Him! Amen!

22. Church in Philadelphia

Many churches—individual denominations or different assemblies—and their individual members are convinced they are the Church of Philadelphia. But only if it were true!

REVELATION 3
[7] And to the angel of the church in Philadelphia write; These things saith he that is holy, he that is true, he that hath the key of David, he that openeth, and no man shutteth; and shutteth, and no man openeth;
[8] I know thy works: behold, I have set before thee an open door, and no man can shut it: for thou hast a little strength, and hast kept my word, and hast not denied my name.
[9] Behold, I will make them of the synagogue of Satan, which say they are Jews, and are not, but do lie; behold, I will

make them to come and worship before thy feet, and to
know that I have loved thee.
[10] Because thou hast kept the word of my patience, I also
will keep thee from the hour of temptation which shall
come upon all the world, to try them that dwell upon the
earth.
[11] Behold, I come quickly: hold that fast which thou hast,
that no man take thy crown.
[12] Him that overcometh will I make a pillar in the temple
of my God, and he shall go no more out: and I will write
upon him the name of my God, and the name of the city of
my God, *which is* new Jerusalem, which cometh down out
of heaven from my God: and *I will write upon him* my new
name.
[13] He that hath an ear, let him hear what the Spirit saith
unto the churches.

This church "hast kept my word" and is often believed to escape the Tribulation times by a previous Rapture, due to the phrase in verse 10: "keep thee from the hour of temptation". This phrase is generally figured to mean "keep out of the hour", and *temptation* is supposed to represent the Tribulation. "Keep thee from the hour" is one of the major justifications for considering a Rapture prior to the Tribulation.

It would be nice if the meaning of *from* were simple and straightforward. Does it really mean *out of*, as held in the pre-Tribulation Rapture view?[14]

John 17
[15] I pray not that thou shouldest take them out of the world,
but that thou shouldest keep them from the evil.

I Corinthians 9
[19] For though I be free from all *men*, yet have I made myself
servant unto all, that I might gain the more.

Galatians 1
[4] Who gave himself for our sins, that he might deliver us
from this present evil world, according to the will of God
and our Father:

II Peter 2
21 For it had been better for them not to have known the way of righteousness, than, after they have known *it*, to turn from the holy commandment delivered unto them.

In these examples, the word *from* definitely does not mean "out of, out of the midst, out from within", but does mean "a preservation from". The term translated to *from* is *ek*. In another instance, *ek* has the same meaning but has been translated four times to *over:*

Revelation 15
2 And I saw as it were a sea of glass mingled with fire: and them that had gotten the victory over the beast, and over his image, and over his mark, and over the number of his name, stand on the sea of glass, having the harps of God.

Two of the most readily available references do not even agree on which term has been translated to the word *from* in Revelation 3:10. One indicates the term is *apo*[15] whereas the other indicates the term is *ek.*[16] Both references agree that *from* is *apo* in Revelation 3:12 in "from my God".

In Revelation 3:12, the use of *apo* indicates an item, or thing, coming from or "away from someone" (in this case, God). This type of usage represents 62 percent of the New Testament translations of *apo*, whereas *out of* represents only about 4.5 percent.

In verse 12, "shall go no more out" has a completely different term translated to *out*. In "down out of heaven", two terms are used for *out:* i.e., *ek* and *the*, meaning "from the". The term *ek* is translated as "of" 47 percent of its uses, "from" 21 percent and "out of" 15 percent.

The idea of "keep out, out from within, or out of the midst of" is not really substantiated by either of the terms in texts used for translation. The idea is relatively weak, and no other supporting Scripture examples have been found.

Regardless of the terms translated, the words provide a weak basis for doctrine.

- The word meanings probably are stretched.
- Different terms are referenced from the translation texts.
- No corroborating Scripture has been identified.

It would not appear wise to use one or two uncertain terms as a major foundation block for doctrine.

There is another portion of the letter to the Church of Philadelphia that should be discussed. Those who "hast kept the word . . . I . . . will keep . . . from the hour of temptation", This temptation is the same temptation as used in "lead us not into temptation".

As mentioned earlier, the temptation is usually considered to be the same as the Tribulation. Where is the justification in Scripture for such an assumption? In the Lord's Prayer, the request is "lead . . . not into temptation," and this is answered (granted) with "keep from . . . temptation"! Believers are spared from temptation, but it is well known that Believers have experienced Tribulation for almost two thousand years! The "temptation . . . shall come upon . . . them that dwell upon the earth":

> REVELATION 3
> 10 Because thou hast kept the word of my patience, I also will keep thee from the hour of temptation, which shall come upon all the world, to try them that dwell upon the earth.

This temptation is for "them that dwell upon the earth", Who are these people? Scripture defines "them that dwell upon the earth" ten times in Revelation as nonbelievers. They are *tried by temptation, kill Believers, not in the book of life, deceived* and they *worship the beast, make image of beast, rejoice over death of GOD's* two witnesses and *admire the beast*:

REVELATION 13
[8] And all that dwell upon the earth shall worship him, whose names are not written in the book of life of the Lamb slain from the foundation of the world.
[12] And he exerciseth all the power of the first beast before him, and causeth the earth and them that dwell therein to worship the first beast, whose deadly wound was healed.
[14] And deceiveth them that dwell on the earth *by means of* those miracles which he had power to do in the sight of the beast; saying to them that dwell on the earth, that they should make an image to the beast, which had the wound by a sword, and did live.

(See also Rev. 6:10; 11:10; 14:6; 17:8.)

The people left after the Rapture are them "that dwell upon the earth" and experience the Wrath of GOD. Remember, Believers experience Tribulation but not Wrath and not temptation. Here, *temptation* is another term for *Wrath*, not *Tribulation.*

A basic message to the Church of Philadelphia is that they will be separated from the nonbelievers and will not experience GOD's Wrath.

23. Come as a Thief?

Lord Jesus Christ often referred to His Coming (coming to gather His elect—the Rapture) as similar to the coming of a thief. However, His Coming as a thief is defined whereby a thief will be in the eyes of the nonbelievers, but not as a thief to Believers!

I THESSALONIANS 5
[4] But ye, brethren, are not in darkness, that that day should overtake you as a thief.

Believers—"ye, brethren"—will not be overtaken "as by a thief" and should not be surprised. It needs to be noted that the subject is the day that will "not overtake" (and surprise) Believers. The Believers are "of the day" and are in light, not in darkness. The darkness refers to a spiritual darkness and it is the nonbelievers who will be surprised:

> I Thessalonians 5
> 3 For when they shall say, Peace and safety; then sudden
> destruction cometh upon them, as travail upon a woman
> with child; and they shall not escape.
> 5 Ye are all the children of light, and the children of the
> day: we are not of the night, nor of darkness.

The above three verses make very definite distinctions between *they, them* and *ye brethren*. The differences between light and darkness are described in Scripture, such as:

> John 3
> 19 And this is the condemnation, that light is come into the
> world, and men loved darkness rather than light, because
> their deeds were evil.
> 20 For every one that doeth evil hateth the light, neither
> cometh to the light, lest his deeds should be reproved.

> I John 1
> 5 This then is the message which we have heard of him,
> and declare unto you, that God is light, and in him is no
> darkness at all.
> 6 If we say that we have fellowship with him, and walk in
> darkness, we lie, and do not the truth:

There will be physical darkness at the time Lord Jesus Christ comes:

> Matthew 24
> 29 Immediately after the tribulation of those days shall the
> sun be darkened, and the moon shall not give her light,
> and the stars shall fall from heaven, and the powers of the
> heavens shall be shaken:

Mark 13
[24] But in those days, after that tribulation, the sun shall be
darkened, and the moon shall not give her light,

And, there will be spiritual darkness when Lord Jesus comes. This is a darkness that should result in no surprise for Believers:

Luke 21
[34] And take heed to yourselves, lest at any time your hearts
be overcharged with surfeiting, and drunkenness, and
cares of this life, and so that day come upon you unawares.
[35] For as a snare shall it come on all them that dwell on the
face of the whole earth.

I Thessalonians 5
[6] Therefore let us not sleep, as *do* others; but let us watch
and be sober.
[7] For they that sleep sleep in the night; and they that be
drunken are drunken in the night.

God's two witnesses will probably be raised at the same time of the Rapture. Those in spiritual darkness will surely be surprised because their celebrations will get ruined and they will have "great fear".

As previously mentioned, if there were a Rapture prior to this time, people would be aware of it and not react with great fear. Scripture has provided an example showing the nonbelievers will be surprised! The fact is that Believers should not be surprised.

The Believers who are "alive and remain" should know the day!

24. Watch! Know Timing!

When Lord Jesus Christ gave the disciples a preview of the Olivet Discourse (Luke 17:22–37), He stated quite clearly that they "shall not see . . . days of the son of man". They would not see the days of His Coming back to earth.

LUKE 17
22 And he said unto the disciples, The days will come, when ye shall desire to see one of the days of the Son of man, and ye shall not see *it*.

During the Olivet Discourse—heard only by Peter, James, John, and Andrew (Mark 13:3)—Lord Jesus Christ told them of no one knowing the day nor hour of His Coming:

MATTHEW 24
36 But of that day and hour knoweth no *man*, no, not the angels of heaven, but my Father only.
42 Watch therefore: for ye know not what hour your Lord doth come.

MATTHEW 25
13 Watch therefore, for ye know neither the day nor the hour wherein the Son of man cometh.

MARK 13
32 But of that day and *that* hour knoweth no man, no, not the angels which are in heaven, neither the Son, but the Father.
33 Take ye heed, watch and pray: for ye know not when the time is.
35 Watch ye therefore: for ye know not when the master of the house cometh, at even, or at midnight, or at the cock-crowing, or in the morning:

These words were given to the disciples, but Jesus Christ also indicated they were meant for everyone:

MARK 13
37 And what I say unto you I say unto all, Watch.

But, John did "see" the Coming and return of Jesus Christ, even if it were in a vision. Is there a contradiction that John was not to see the days? First, there is a possibility John did not hear the preview to the Discourse, because he may have been in another village:

> LUKE 10
> [1] After these things the Lord appointed other seventy also, and sent them two and two before his face into every city and place, whither he himself would come.

In addition, Jesus Christ later made John an exception:

> JOHN 21
> [22] Jesus saith unto him, If I will that he tarry till I come, what *is that* to thee? follow thou me.
> [23] Then went this saying abroad among the brethren, that that disciple should not die: yet Jesus said not unto him, He shall not die; but, If I will that he tarry till I come, what *is that* to thee?

It is obvious that the other disciples did not see the Lord Jesus Christ's Coming and return. They all died.

Back to the Olivet Discourse! The quoted Scripture contains quite a few statements to "Watch" for His Coming and that "no one knows the day or hour of that coming". To *watch* is recorded seven times in the Discourse. Even if the recorded statements contain some duplications of Jesus Christ's words, it appears that He stated *watch* at least six times! In other words, *watch*!

Why should Believers (they are part of *everyone)* watch if they have been removed from earth in a previous gathering of the elect, a previous Rapture? Why watch for the Coming of Lord Jesus Christ if the Rapture timing is secret and there is no clue to its timing? The Olivet Discourse is very descriptive of the events answering questions about "when and what is the sign of His coming":

> MATTHEW 24
> [3] And as he sat upon the mount of Olives, the disciples came unto him privately, saying, Tell us, when shall these

things be? and what *shall be* the sign of thy coming, and of the end of the world?

MARK 13
[4] Tell us, when shall these things be? and what *shall be* the sign when all these things shall be fulfilled?

LUKE 21
[28] And when these things begin to come to pass, then look up, and lift up your heads; for your redemption draweth nigh.
[31] So likewise ye, when ye see these things come to pass, know ye that the kingdom of God is nigh at hand.

It seems that the Olivet Discourse is fairly clear about the events prior to His coming—prior to the Rapture. Also, it would seem to indicate the Rapture will not be a secret surprise. But the Discourse includes six statements to the effect that no one knows the day, hour, or time when Jesus Christ will come—the resurrection and Rapture—for His elect. Not knowing the time appears to be in conflict with Jesus Christ's instructions to "watch . . . know that it is nigh". Not knowing is also in contradiction to the information given to Daniel about his resurrection and Rapture timing. Yet, knowing the timing appears to be in conflict with "no one knows".

The timing should be known and will be known by those not in spiritual darkness but spiritually awake! The idea that the Rapture timing will be known is far from a popular concept; it is usually passed off as totally non-Scriptural and heretical. However, if the timing is not to be known, the aforementioned conflicts exist. GOD did not provide a Scripture with conflicting information!

A study of the term translated to *know* shows the timing is to be known. More accurately, the study should be of each usage by Lord Jesus Christ of the terms *know not, not knowing, knoweth no (man), know ye not, if ye had known, knowest not now, knowest not*, etc. There are at least eleven different terms translated to the English word *know.* Jesus Christ used *oida* with a negative (i.e., *no, not)* thirty-two times in the New Testament.[17,18]

Oida **means "to know" in the present tense with the present meaning and suggests fullness of meaning.**[19] When Jesus Christ used the negative with *oida*, He indicated "not knowing at the specific time when spoken". The usage does not indicate *not being able to know, shouldn't know, couldn't know, wouldn't ever know* nor *can't know!*

Eight of the times when Jesus Christ used a term equivalent to *you oida not*, the knowledge did become known at a later time. Examples are Mark 10:38; Luke 9:55; John 4:32; 8:55; 15:15 and:

> MATTHEW 20
> 22 Jesus answered and said, Ye know not what ye ask. Are ye able to drink of the cup that I shall drink of, and to be baptized with the baptism that I am baptized with? They say unto him, We are able.

> MARK 4
> 13 And he said unto them, Know ye not this parable? and how then will ye know all parables?

> JOHN 13
> 7 Jesus answered and said unto him, What I do thou knowest not now; but thou shalt know hereafter.

Where the above Scripture states "then will ye know" and "thou shalt know", a different term is used for "know": *ginosko*. Jesus Christ used the metaphors of "drink of the cup" and "baptism" to indicate His respective Crucifixion and burial. These words were spoken to a couple of His disciples within a week or so prior to those major events. They did not know what was meant at the time those words were spoken. Some time later, the disciples and other Believers did know (understand) what He had said.

Thirteen of the times when Jesus Christ used the *oida* term with a negative, the "knowing" should or could be known:

Mark 12:24; Luke 23:34; John 7:28; 8:19, 55; 12:35; 14:17; 15:21; Revelation 3:17. In these next two examples, Jesus Christ said basically, "You don't know [*oida*: now, while it is spoken], but you will come to know [*ginosko*: fully understand] at a later time":

> MATTHEW 22
> 29 Jesus answered and said unto them, Ye do err, not knowing the scriptures, nor the power of God.

> JOHN 4
> 22 Ye worship ye know not what: we know what we worship: for salvation is of the Jews.

In the two examples just quoted, "not knowing the Scriptures" certainly should not be taken to mean the Scripture could not/cannot be understood! In the second example, Jesus Christ was saying, "Ye know not what [while he is speaking], [but] we know what [while he is speaking]".

There is no indication that *oida not* should mean "knowing" is not to be. Rather, there is the implication that knowledge will, or should, occur in the future.

Three times Jesus Christ said, "I know you not", referring to "those who work iniquity" (Matt. 25:12; Luke 13:25, 27). His statements of "I know [*oida*] you not" should not be understood to mean He could not or would not know you. The statement is one of disapproval for iniquity. Righteousness, justice and repentance would undoubtedly have replaced iniquity, through Grace, and He would have "known you".

Jesus Christ used the term where future *knowing* might be unlikely, but it referred to animals, which could have been taught. *Oida* in both cases:

> JOHN 10
> 4 And when he putteth forth his own sheep, he goeth before them, and the sheep follow him: for they know his voice.
> 5 And a stranger will they not follow, but will flee from him; for they know not the voice of strangers.

In another situation, Lord Jesus used the *oida* term again where eventual knowledge would seem unlikely. This was: "The seed should spring and grow up, he knoweth not how" (Mark 4:27). This is a statement in part of the parables about the sower and various seeds. These parables were explained, and the disciples (then) understood in the context intended—the sowing of the Word—hearing about the kingdom of GOD.

Six (recorded) times Jesus Christ used the term *oida* in the Olivet Discourse concerning the time of His coming (Matt. 24:36, 42; 25:13; Mark 13:32, 33, 35). The timing was not known when spoken and is not yet known.

Some uses of the same term by others than Jesus Christ are:

JOHN 20
9 For as yet they knew not the Scripture, that he must rise again from the dead.

JOHN 21
4 But when the morning was now come, Jesus stood on the shore; but the disciples knew not that it was Jesus.

Before Jesus Christ was taken up into a cloud and into heaven, He reiterated to the disciples that they were not to know the time of His return. Here, the *not . . . to know* is not the term *oida*, but a different term: *ginosko*:

ACTS 1
7 And he said unto them, It is not for you to know the times or the seasons, which the Father hath put in his own power.

Not one instance has been found in the New Testament record where Lord Jesus Christ used the term *oida not* (or similar term) where "not know" meant *would not, could not* nor *will not be known*!

It should be noted that the last information from Lord Jesus Christ concerning knowing or not knowing the timing of His Coming is a conditional statement:

> Revelation 3
> [3] Remember therefore how thou hast received and heard, and hold fast, and repent. If therefore thou shalt not watch, I will come on thee as a thief, and thou shalt not know what hour I will come upon thee.

A different term for *know* is used here: *ginosko*. The statement is in Jesus Christ's letter to the church at Sardis and the verse just quoted is the main message of that letter: "Watch and you will know the hour"! Jesus Christ would not have made the statement if His Coming were to be of unknown or secret timing.

Unfortunately, most churches in the United States are not watching. They don't care or don't want to care. Or they have been taught that they can't understand what to watch for, it won't do any good to watch or watching for a sudden surprise is futile. This is a sad situation, very sad, and it is not Scriptural.

To think that Believers will not, or cannot, know the timing of Lord Jesus Christ's Coming for His elect does not fit with Scripture:

- It does not fit with the instructions to *watch*.
- It does not fit with His describing events and then indicating redemption "is nigh".
- It contradicts Jesus Christ's own statement to the churches.
- Nor does the idea fit that Jesus Christ will return like a thief for Believers; the day of His Coming will only overtake nonbelievers as a thief.

It does not fit Scripture that Rapture timing cannot be known when there are many passages concerning end-time events and time periods. Daniel contains at least eight such statements of time periods and Revelation contains at least ten time period statements. (Revelation does have more times given. They are discussed later):

Daniel 7:25	Daniel 12:11	Revelation 11:3
Daniel 8:13	Daniel 12:12	Revelation 11:9
Daniel 9:26	Revelation 2:10	Revelation 12:6
Daniel 9:27	Revelation 8:1	Revelation 12:14
Daniel 11:24	Revelation 9:5	Revelation 13:5
Daniel 12:7	Revelation 11:2	Revelation 17:12

The timing of Jesus Christ's first Coming to earth was predicted through Daniel. Various analyses have been given, and they conclude that the prophecy was fulfilled to the day![20,21] If Israel had really been able to understand the Word of God, the timing of His first Coming could have been recognized!

Surely, these time periods and events are in the holy Scripture to be used and understood!

Those who are alive and remain should know the day when Lord Jesus comes for His elect—the Rapture!

Watch!

Chapter Five

25. Daniel's Prophecies Fulfilled?

Daniel's prophecies—visions—have many details that appear to have been fulfilled. This is particularly true of his last vision (Dan. 11–12). It is easy to conclude they have been fulfilled up through Daniel 11:35 because so many details can be related to historical events.[22] The idea is that the end-time events will pick up with Daniel 11:36. It is worth examining what may have been fulfilled and what may be foreshadows of prophecies that actually have not been fulfilled.

In Daniel's second vision, the male goat is often thought to have been fulfilled by Alexander the Great and the Grecian Kingdom, around 300 B.C.:

> DANIEL 8
> 5 And as I was considering, behold, an he goat came from the west on the face of the whole earth, and touched not the ground: and the goat *had* a notable horn between his eyes.

Alexander did not travel "on the face of the whole earth". Although he covered a great deal of known civilization at the time, he did not travel the whole earth. Nor did Alexander travel "and touched not the ground". He rode in chariots, but he still had to touch the ground. Fulfillment would require something like an aircraft, rocket or space vehicle in place of a chariot.

Historically, a "great horn was broken" is supposed to have been fulfilled by Alexander:

DANIEL 8
[8] Therefore the he goat waxed very great: and when he was strong, the great horn was broken; and for it came up four notable ones toward the four winds of heaven.

After Alexander died, his kingdom was split into four parts, with each one under each of his generals. The kingdom where the split is described and the antichrist arises then became Thrace, Macedonia, Syria and Egypt:

DANIEL 8
[9] And out of one of them came forth a little horn, which waxed exceeding great, toward the south, and toward the east, and toward the pleasant *land*.

DANIEL 11
[4] And when he shall stand up, his kingdom shall be broken, and shall be divided toward the four winds of heaven; and not to his posterity, nor according to his dominion which he ruled: for his kingdom shall be plucked up, even for others besides those.

Division into four kingdoms would be "four kingdoms toward the four winds of heaven and his kingdom divided . . . four winds . . . kingdom plucked up". Alexander's "kingdom divided toward the four winds of heaven" did not really occur. The "four winds of heaven" refer to supernatural events by GOD:

DANIEL 7
[2] Daniel spake and said, I saw in my vision by night, and, behold, the four winds of the heaven strove upon the great sea.

EZEKIEL 37
[9] Then said he unto me, Prophesy unto the wind, prophesy, son of man, and say to the wind, Thus saith the Lord GOD; Come from the four winds, 0 breath, and breathe upon these slain, that they may live.

ZECHARIAH 2
[6] Ho, ho, *come forth,* and flee from the land of the north,
saith the LORD: for I have spread you abroad as the four
winds of the heaven, saith the LORD.

JEREMIAH 49
[36] And upon Elam will I bring the four winds from the
four quarters of heaven, and will scatter them toward all
those winds; and there shall be no nation whither the
outcasts of Elam shall not come.

MATTHEW 24
[31] And he shall send his angels with a great sound of a
trumpet, and they shall gather together his elect from the
four winds, from one end of heaven to the other.

History has not shown any scattering nor gathering in the context of four winds of heaven. Nor was Alexander's kingdom "plucked up". Daniel used a term translated to "plucked up" which is also used to describe GOD's activities:

JEREMIAH 31
[40] And the whole valley of the dead bodies, and of the ashes,
and all the fields unto the brook of Kidron, unto the corner
of the horse gate toward the east, *shall be* holy unto the
LORD; it shall not be plucked up, nor thrown down any
more for ever.

Ezekiel 19
[12] But she was plucked up in fury, she was cast down to
the ground, and the east wind dried up her fruit: her strong
rods were broken and withered; the fire consumed them.

II CHRONICLES 7
[20] Then will I pluck them up by the roots out of my land
which I have given them; and this house, which I have
sanctified for my name, will I cast out of my sight, and
will make it *to be* a proverb and a byword among all
nations.

The kingdom was not dispersed rapidly, nor even over a period of time. The people and their descendants remain today and were not spread into other countries, such as has happened to Israel.

Scripture also indicates "a king of fierce countenance"—the antichrist—will arise during the "later time of their kingdom":

> DANIEL 8
> [23] And in the latter time of their kingdom, when the transgressors are come to the full, a king of fierce countenance, and understanding dark sentences, shall stand up.

This would indicate the four kingdoms exist, including the kings, at the time the antichrist will arise. But the kings haven't been around for many years.

If Antiochus Epiphanes (around 170 B.C.) were the antichrist, then he didn't "cast down . . . stars to the ground" nor was he "great even to the host of heaven". He didn't fulfill prophecy:

> DANIEL 8
> [10] And it waxed great, *even* to the host of heaven; and it cast down *some* of the host and of the stars to the ground, and stamped upon them.

Daniel's last vision has also been used (supposedly) to show Alexander in history:

> DANIEL 11
> [3] And a mighty king shall stand up, that shall rule with great dominion, and do according to his will.
> [4] And when he shall stand up, his kingdom shall be broken, and shall be divided toward the four winds of heaven; and not to his posterity, nor according to his dominion which he ruled: for his kingdom shall be plucked up, even for others beside those.

These events cannot be descriptions of Alexander. They are parenthetical and present a view of a future antichrist:

> DANIEL 8
> [25] And through his policy also he shall cause craft to prosper in his hand; and he shall magnify *himself* in his heart, and by peace shall destroy many: he shall also stand up against the Prince of princes; but he shall be broken without hand.

> DANIEL 11
> [6] And in the end of years they shall join themselves together; for the king's daughter of the south shall come to the king of the north to make an agreement: but she shall not retain the power of the arm; neither shall he stand, nor his arm: but she shall be given up, and they that brought her, and he that begat her, and he that strengthened her in *these* times.

> DANIEL 11
> [36] And the king shall do according to his will; and he shall exalt himself, and magnify himself above every god, and shall speak marvellous things against the God of gods, and shall prosper till the indignation be accomplished: for that that is determined shall be done.
> [45] And he shall plant the tabernacles of his palace between the seas in the glorious holy mountain; yet he shall come to his end, and none shall help him.

Even the phrase "when he shall stand up" (Dan. 11:4) is a clue that the entire vision is not presented in complete chronological sequence and would not represent Alexander. The timing of *when* is "when he shall stand up" and has no connection to previous events nor to events immediately following.

It should be remembered that Jesus Christ's words to Daniel were in answer to his concerns about Jerusalem and Judah. The words relate directly to the time periods of "confirm the covenant" and the "seventieth week"! (Dan. 9:24–27). The historical events occurred over a period of approximately

365 years. In the future, nations with modern equipment such as tanks, missiles, aircraft, communications, etc., will be at war and major changes will occur as "a flood":

> DANIEL 9
> [26] And after threescore and two weeks shall Messiah be cut off, but not for himself: and the people of the prince that shall come shall destroy the city and the sanctuary; and the end thereof *shall be* with a flood, and unto the end of the war desolations are determined.

> DANIEL 11
> [22] And with the arms of a flood shall they be overflown from before him, and shall be broken; yea, also the prince of the covenant.

That Daniel's prophecies have not been fulfilled is indicated because he was specifically told they would be "at the time of the end . . . the end . . . consummation . . . latter days . . . end of years . . . time of the end . . . time of the end . . . the end . . . time of the end . . . end of the days" (Dan. 8: 17, 19; 9:27; 10:14; 11:6, 35, 40; 12: 4, 8–9, 13). Also, the general context of the prophecies refer to subjects such as "judgment . . . whole earth . . . everlasting kingdom . . . many days . . . indignation accomplished . . . people delivered . . . everlasting . . . finished" (Dan. 7:9, 11, 22–23, 26–27; 8:5, 10, 25–26; 9:24; 11:36; 12:1–2, 7). There are at least twenty-six indications that Daniel prophesied about the end times and not only about events of 2500 years ago!

The historical events that appear to have been fulfilled by Daniel's prophecies are fantastic foreshadows of coming events!

Daniel's visions are yet to come! Watch!

Understanding that the prophecies of Daniel are yet to come gives meaning to Lord Jesus Christ's words: "spoken by Daniel the prophet . . . (whoso readeth, let him understand)" as given in Matthew 24:15 and Mark 13:4.

26. Antichrist Confirms Covenant?

The antichrist appears in Daniel's last vision as a "vile person". This is back-traced from subsequent details through grammar usage of the subjects and subject pronouns:

> DANIEL 11
> 21 And in his estate shall stand up a vile person, to whom
> they shall not give the honour of the kingdom: but he shall
> come in peaceably, and obtain the kingdom by flatteries.
> 22 And with the arms of a flood shall they be overflown
> from before him, and shall be broken; yea, also the prince
> of the covenant.

The "prince of the covenant" is *broken:* that means ruined, dominated, crushed or shattered by the vile person—the antichrist. Yet many explanations of end-time events indicate that the antichrist will be the one confirming the covenant and allowing Israel to have sacrifices and worship services. If the antichrist breaks the "prince of the covenant", then he must break himself because they would then be one and the same individual—not too likely!

Why the antichrist would make the covenant is not explained. The idea that the antichrist *confirms the covenant* comes from:

> DANIEL 9
> 26 And after threescore and two weeks shall Messiah be
> cut off, but not for himself: and the people of the prince
> that shall come shall destroy the city and the sanctuary;
> and the end thereof *shall be* with a flood, and unto the end
> of the war desolations are determined.
> 27 And he shall confirm the covenant with many for one
> week: and in the midst of the week he shall cause the
> sacrifice and the oblation to cease, and for the
> overspreading of abominations he shall make *it* desolate,

> even until the consummation, and that determined shall be poured upon the desolate.

It is "the people" who will destroy the city and the sanctuary—"the people of the prince". The *he* is the prince, as indicated by grammar. If this "prince" is the antichrist, then he would be "breaking" himself (Dan. 11:22). However, if the phrase "prince that shall come" is referring to Satan, then it is "the people" who are doing the dictate of Satan—Satan confirming the covenant through people.

Satan is a prince who will come to earth:

> Revelation 12
> [9] And the great dragon was cast out, that old serpent, called the Devil, and Satan, which deceiveth the whole world: he was cast out into the earth, and his angels were cast out with him.

It doesn't seem possible that the antichrist will be confirming the covenant. History shows that a high priest (not Antiochus Epiphanes) was deposed as a prince of the covenant during foreshadowing events of history.[23] The antichrist won't be the one to confirm the covenant. Nor will the "king of the north" confirm the covenant, as is sometimes suggested. However, the antichrist will make a "league with the prince of the covenant" after "the prince of the covenant is broken":

> Daniel 11
> [22] And with the arms of a flood shall they be overflown from before him, and shall be broken; yea, also the prince of the covenant.
> [23] And after the league *made* with him he shall work deceitfully: for he shall come up, and shall become strong with a small people.

The antichrist does not confirm the covenant!

27. Antichrist and Seal One

The antichrist does not confirm the covenant, and he is not likely to be the rider of the white horse of Seal One in the Book of Revelation! Almost all interpretations of Revelation and books written about the end times indicate this rider is the antichrist and Seal One represents a deceiver or false Christ being turned loose on the earth. This rider is much more likely to be the Word of God and not the antichrist![24]

Scripture shows this to be the case when descriptions about this rider in different situations are compared. At issue are descriptive terms such as *white horse, he that sat on him* (white horse), *bow, crown and crowns, conquering and to conquer, The Word of God, out of his mouth goeth a sharp sword, sword of him*. Most of these terms, and variations of them, are found in the First Seal and the battle of Armageddon as described in Revelation:

> REVELATION 6
> 2 And I saw, and behold a white horse: and he that sat on
> him had a bow; and a crown was given unto him: and he
> went forth conquering, and to conquer.
>
> REVELATION 19
> 11 And I saw heaven opened, and behold a white horse;
> and he that sat upon him was called Faithful and True,
> and in righteousness he doth judge and make war.
> 12 His eyes were as a flame of fire, and on his head were
> many crowns; and he had a name written, that no man
> knew, but he himself.
> 13 And he *was* clothed with a vesture dipped in blood: and
> his name is called The Word of God.
> 15 And out of his mouth goeth a sharp sword, that with it
> he should smite the nations: and he shall rule them with a
> rod of iron: and he treadeth the winepress of the fierceness
> and wrath of Almighty God.
> 19 And I saw the beast, and the kings of the earth, and their
> armies, gathered together to make war against him that
> sat on the horse, and against his army.

> 21 And the remnant were slain with the sword of him that sat upon the horse, which *sword* proceeded out of his mouth: and all the fowls were filled with their flesh.

Each word in Scripture is significant: *white* is used sixteen times in Revelation to indicate cleanliness, purity or holiness (Rev. 1:14; 2:17; 3:4–5, 18; 4:4; 6:11; 7:9, 13–14; 14:14; 15:6; 19:8, 14; 20:11). The colors of the horses seen in the following three Seals are descriptive of the rider's characteristics: i.e., red, black, and pale representing war, famine, and death (Rev. 6:4–5, 8). White is not a description of the antichrist's character. Those in heaven—creatures, elders, angels, Christ and John—would not have envisioned a defiled horse ridden by the antichrist to be white.

The rider is specifically identified as the Word of God: i.e., Jesus Christ, the Spirit of Christ, or the everlasting gospel. We read in Revelation 6:2: "white horse . . . and he that sat on him had a bow. . .". Jeremiah 9:3 states, "And they bend their tongues like their *bow* . . .", showing a bow represents power behind the tongue and behind any words proceeding from the tongue or mouth. Habbakuk is much more specific and indicates the *bow* and *word* as being synonymous:

> HABBAKUK 3
> 9 Thy bow was made quite naked, *according* to the oaths of the tribes, *even* thy word. Selah. Thou didst cleave the earth with rivers.

The rider of the white horse is the Word of God, and His power is in His tongue/mouth/word/sharp sword/sword, which are also represented by a bow: "behold a white horse; and he that sat upon him . . . called the Word of God . . . and out his mouth goeth a sharp sword . . . And the remnant were slain with the sword of him that sat upon the horse, which . . . proceeded out of his mouth"(Rev. 19:11,13, 15, 21). The rider is, or carries, the Word of God.

The rider has a crown and crowns. In the First Seal, the rider is given a crown: "A *crown* was given unto him. . . ."

Later, the rider has many crowns: ". . . and on his head were *many crowns. . .*". These references are not about the same crowns. The crown of the First Seal represents victory as associated with "conquering and to conquer". The "many crowns" represents royalty. Both types of crowns belong only to Jesus Christ!

The rider of the white horse is "conquering and to conquer" and will be totally victorious: ". . . a white horse: and he that sat on him . . . went forth conquering and to conquer . . ." (Rev. 6:2). *Conquering* and *conquer* are the same basic word meaning "victory, overcome, prevail" as used in Revelation 5:5: ". . . Lion . . . of Judah . . . Root of David, hath prevailed to open the book. . .".

Conquering is present active and certainly describes the activity of Jesus Christ, the Word! *To conquer* is aorist subjunctive active—i.e., not time dependent but eventual reality of the event. The final reality of victory belongs only to Jesus Christ. The antichrist will have only some temporary successes and not total victory! Revelation 19:11–21 gives a vivid account of that rider upon a white horse and His total victory!

Collective descriptions of the rider upon the white horse further demonstrate the oneness of the rider in Revelation 6 and 19. The one short verse of the First Seal identifies characteristics of the rider and his horse, which are further described in Revelation 19. Without attempting any statistical analysis, the possibilities are extremely remote that the rider in Seal One can be anyone other than the Word of God.

The common characteristics are:

- Rider of a white horse
- The white horse represents purity and holiness
- Rider is identified as the Word of God or having the Word
- Rider uses mouth/word/bow/sword as power
- Rider has a "crown" and "crowns" belonging only to Christ

- Rider is conquering
- Rider will totally conquer as an eventual reality

None of the above characteristics belong to the antichrist!

Jesus Christ talked about false prophets, false christs, and deceivers in the Olivet Discourse. Such statements are recorded ten times (Matt. 24:4–5,11,23–24; Mark 13:5–6,21–22; Luke 21:8). He also talked about the gospel going forth prior to the end coming (Matt. 24:14; Mark 13:10) and made the specific point that the first thing to occur would be:

MARK 13
10 And the gospel must first be published among all nations.

The first thing is publication (preach, herald, proclaim) of the gospel among the nations. The deceivers and false prophets/Christs are not first. The gospel is first. The bow, which is the Word of God, is first, represented by the First Seal.

The Second Seal contains a specific clue that the First Seal would not be the antichrist. The Second Seal indicates: ". . . the second seal . . . horse that was red . . . to take peace from the earth". A key phrase is "take peace from the earth". If the antichrist were active, or started activities, during Seal One, it is highly unlikely there could be peace on earth when the Second Seal starts:

REVELATION 6
3 And when he had opened the second seal, I heard the second beast say, Come and see.
4 And there went out another horse *that was* red: and *power* was given to him that sat thereon to take peace from the earth, and that they should kill one another: and there was given unto him a great sword.

For the Scripture statement to hold true, there must be peace on earth prior to the opening of the Second Seal. There would be peace due to the First Seal and not the antichrist.

The Second Seal also contains another clue that the First Seal does not represent the antichrist: ". . . The second seal . . . horse that was red . . . that should kill one another . . ." In the Olivet Discourse, Jesus Christ describes this seal as "nation shall rise against nation, and kingdom against kingdom. . . All these are the beginning of sorrows. . .":

> MATTHEW 24
> 5 For many shall come in my name, saying, I am Christ; and shall deceive many.
> 6 And ye shall hear of wars and rumours of wars: see that ye be not troubled: for all *these things* must come to pass, but the end is not yet.
> 7 For nation shall rise against nation, and kingdom against kingdom: and there shall be famines, and pestilences, and earthquakes, in divers places.
> 8 All these *are* the beginning of sorrows.

The other key phrase is "beginning of sorrows". Since it is the beginning, then the First Seal could not previously have resulted in any sorrows such as would be the case with the antichrist.

The word *sorrows* is the same word used in I Thessalonians 5:3 for *travail*: ". . . say Peace and safety . . . destruction cometh . . . as *travail* . . . they shall not escape. . .". *Sorrows* is used instead of *travail* only because it is plural. The meaning seems to be "beginning of travail(s)".

The beginning of *sorrows* or *travails* is the Second Seal, not the First Seal. Again, the First Seal will not be the antichrist. At least seven valid reasons have been presented to why the First Seal is not representative of the antichrist.

The First Seal must be symbolic of the Word of God!

28. Build a Temple?

Most discussions about the end times include statements that a Temple will be required and will be a significant sign of end times. This Temple will be built to accommodate sacrifices, offerings, and worship during the covenant time period. In addition, this will be the Temple that will be described at the time the antichrist "sits in the temple showing himself that he is God".

There is no place in Scripture that indicates a Temple will be built, used or needed: at least no place in Scripture according to the "original" languages. Even in English New Testaments, the words translated to "Temple" (during end times) are where the original languages mean "tabernacle" or "holy of holies":

> II Thessalonians 2
> [4] Who opposeth and exalteth himself above all that is called God, or that is worshipped; so that he as God sitteth in the temple of God, shewing himself that he is God.

The holy of holies was the innermost part of the tabernacle, an elaborate tent-type of portable structure that was used for almost five hundred years. The same word for *holy of holies* is used in Revelation twenty times. Every usage, considering the overall context, means "holy of holies". (Some Bible versions use the word *shrine.*)

The point is, according to Scripture, a Temple is not mentioned in the prophecies of end times. The holy of holies may be in a tabernacle, and it is this idea that is actually in Scripture.

In all the Scripture references about a sanctuary, Temple or tabernacle relating to end-time activities, the Hebrew or Greek words used refer specifically to tabernacles, consecrated holy thing, booth, hut, or holy of holies. The Hebrew or Greek words for *Temple* (buildings, courts and sacred ground) are not used.

The Scripture mentions an outer court and Temple, which would imply there will be a Temple:

> Revelation 11
> [1] And there was given me a reed like unto a rod: and the

angel stood, saying, Rise, and measure the temple of God, and the altar, and them that worship therein.
[2] But the court which is without the temple leave out, and measure it not; for it is given unto the Gentiles: and the holy city shall they tread under foot forty *and* two months.

A quick glance would leave the definite idea there will be a Temple and an outer court. The term translated to *Temple* means the "dwelling place of God" or "holy of holies". Only one human (a priest) was allowed in the holy of holies, and only once a year. The *them* indicates more than one person. The "measuring . . . them in the temple of God . . ." is measuring (not counting numbers) of Believers. Christ is in the Believers, and the Body of Christ is the temple of God. The statements about a Temple and court do not represent a physical Temple.

A few other examples are presented showing a Temple may not be built. Daniel used two different words for *sanctuary* in the prophecies about end times. These two words are completely different than the one he used when referring to the Temple in Jerusalem. One of the words appears in:

DANIEL 8
[11] Yea, he magnified *himself* even to the prince of the host, and by him the daily *sacrifice* was taken away, and the place of his sanctuary was cast down.

Here, Daniel uses a word for *sanctuary* (not *Temple*) meaning "tabernacle, consecrated thing or consecrated place". The same usage appears in Daniel 9:26.

The second word Daniel uses is in:

DANIEL 8
[13] Then I heard one saint speaking, and another saint said unto that certain *saint* which spake, How long *shall be* the vision *concerning* the daily *sacrifice*, and the transgression of desolation, to give both the sanctuary and the host to be trodden under foot?

This second term for *sanctuary* means "holy thing, holy of holies" also used in Daniel 8:14 and 11:31. Daniel emphasizes the differences even more by using another term when the antichrist "plants the tabernacles":

> DANIEL 11
> 45 And he shall plant the tabernacles of his palace between the seas in the glorious holy mountain; yet he shall come to his end, and none shall help him.

When the antichrist "sits in the Temple showing himself that he is God" (II Thes. 2:4), the term for *Temple* means "holy of holies", as mentioned previously. When the antichrist (identified as the first beast) blasphemes GOD's Temple, it will probably be a booth, hut, or tabernacle and not a true Temple:

> REVELATION 13
> 6 And he opened his mouth in blasphemy against God, to blaspheme his name, and his tabernacle, and them that dwell in heaven.

It is difficult to imagine an egotistical antichrist would "show himself that he is God" in a tabernacle-type structure. However, we don't know what kind of conditions will exist in Jerusalem at the time (probably considerable destruction), and a tabernacle may be all that is available.

It is possible that a complete Temple could be built during the end times, but don't count on it. Scripture (almost very pointedly) avoids using of the word *Temple*, and it likely won't happen.

There will be a holy of holies, probably in a tabernacle.

29. Revived Roman Empire?

Most end-time concepts present the antichrist's kingdom as a revived Roman Empire. This usually has been described as the European Economic Community (Common Market) with ten nations and the antichrist coming from one of those nations. There are several things that should be considered:

1. The EEC (European Economic Community) has 14–16 members, not 10.
2. The EEC represents only one-quarter of the old Roman Empire land area, and represents less than one-fifth of the land area controlled by all the previous kingdoms described by Daniel.
3. The antichrist comes from Assyria, not Europe.

Isaiah 10

5 O Assyrian, the rod of mine anger, and the staff in their hand is mine indignation.

6 I will send him against an hypocritical nation, and against the people of my wrath will I give him a charge, to take the spoil, and to take the prey, and to tread them down like the mire of the streets.

12 Wherefore it shall come to pass, *that,* when the Lord hath performed his whole work upon mount Zion and on Jerusalem, I will punish the fruit of the stout heart of the king of Assyria, and the glory of his high looks.

13 For he saith, By the strength of my hand I have done *it,* and by my wisdom; for I am prudent: and I have removed the bounds of the people, and have robbed their treasures, and I have put down the inhabitants like a valiant *man:*

Descriptions of the last kingdom (of man and Satan) point out it is different than the previous kingdoms:

Daniel 7

7 After this I saw in the night visions, and behold a fourth beast, dreadful and terrible, and strong exceedingly; and it had great iron teeth: it devoured and brake in pieces, and stamped the residue with the feet of it: and it *was* diverse from all the beasts that *were* before it; and it had ten horns.

> [19] Then I would know the truth of the fourth beast, which was diverse from all the others, exceeding dreadful, whose teeth *were of* iron, and his nails *of* brass; *which* devoured, brake in pieces, and stamped the residue with his feet;

The fourth kingdom (the antichrist as the beast) will rule over the "whole earth":

> DANIEL 7
> [23] Thus he said, The fourth beast shall be the fourth kingdom upon earth, which shall be diverse from all kingdoms, and shall devour the whole earth, and shall tread it down, and break it in pieces.

Being diverse from the others probably refers to its characteristics more than anything; the other kingdoms had some commonality in the areas controlled, but their general characteristics were distinctly different.

A chart of comparisons is presented only to show an intertwining of old empire characteristics into the fourth kingdom, the kingdom of the antichrist and the beast. This fourth kingdom will have all the characteristics of previous kingdoms (see Chart 11).

Israel is in the middle of the land areas controlled by the previous empires, almost exactly in the center of the total area affected. Most of the antichrist's initial activities should be in these areas. Then, as the beast he will rule over the whole earth.

Europe had little or no influence in the previous empires—actually not even involved except in the latter years of Rome. It seems difficult to identify any of the European nations as the ten nations from which the antichrist will come. This is even more unlikely if the antichrist is an Assyrian leader or of Assyrian descent.

Now, after all the discussions about a revived Roman Empire, it must be pointed out that Daniel mentioned a "third kingdom of brass which shall bear rule over all the earth":

Daniel 2
39 And after thee shall arise another kingdom inferior to thee, and another third kingdom of brass, which shall bear rule over all the earth.

The existence of such a third kingdom has not yet been fulfilled—no human kingdom has yet had rule over all the earth. Why look for the fourth beast and fourth kingdom when the third kingdom has not yet appeared?

CHART #11

MAIN KINGDOMS OF MAN

KINGDOM CHARACTERISTICS	KINGDOM REPRESENTED	SYMBOLISM	CHARACTERISTICS IN LAST KINGDOM	SYMBOLISM IN LAST KINGDOM	REFERENCES
#1 Gold	Babylon	Rich			Dan 2:32
Winged		Covering			Dan 7:4
Lion		King	Mouth of Lion	Authority	Dan 7:4; Rev 13:2
Man's heart		A man			Dan 7:4
#2 Silver	Medo-Persia	Mass of Wealth			Dan 2:32
Bear		Crushing	Feet of Bear	Crushing	Dan 7:5; Rev. 13:2
3 ribs between teeth		Devouring			Dan 7:5
Ram w/2 horns	Strength				Dan 8:3
#3 Brass	Greece	Mixture	Nails of brass	Tear apart, breaks	Dan 2:23; 7:19
Leopard		Swift	Body of leopard	Swift	Dan 7:6; Rev 13:2
4 Wings		Covering	Rule over all earth	Impure nature	Dan 7:6; Dan 2:39
4 Heads		Divided			Dan 7:6
Male goat		Wicked			Dan 8:5-7
One horn (broken)					Dan 8:8
4 new horns	Divided Greece				Dan 8:8
little horn		Antichrist			Dan 8:9
#4 Iron	Man, Antichrist		Strong,non-bending	Strong,non-bending	Dan 2:40
Iron & clay	and Satan	Strong	Part Strong, Part Broken	Part Strong, Part Broken	Dan 2:41,42
Iron teeth		Divided	Devouring	Devouring	Dan 7:7,19
Ten horns/crowns			Ten kingdoms (local)	Political & Military Authority	Dan 7:7; Rev 13:1
11th horn eyes of man speaks great things		Antichrist 1st Beast	Antichrist uproots 3 horns • represented by a man • claims to be God	Accomplished by a man Blasphemy Blasphemy	Dan 7:8; 20 Dan 7:8 Dan 7:8, 20; Rev 13:6
Seven heads Ten horns		Blasphemy	Religious System (2ndBeast) Ten kings (world wide)	 Gather for Armageddon	Rev 17:3 Rev 17:12-14

Chapter Six

30. Antichrist Killed and Then Lives

Although a number of time periods and times of specific events have been identified and shown on charts, total relationships are not yet established. More information is needed to finalize the total program. One such item is when the antichrist is "wounded to death and healed":

> REVELATION 13
> 3 And I saw one of his heads as it were wounded to death; and his deadly wound was healed: and all the world wondered after the beast.

The timing of this event was prophesied by Daniel. Daniel had learned of a three and one-half year period prior to "scattering the holy people". He was also aware of a three and one-half year increment when the antichrist would "wear out the saints and they shall be given unto his hand":

> DANIEL 12
> 7 And I heard the man clothed in linen, which *was* upon the waters of the river, when he held up his right hand and his left hand unto heaven, and sware by him that liveth for ever that *it shall be* for a time, times, and an half; and when he shall have accomplished to scatter the power of the holy people, all these *things* shall be finished.

> DANIEL 7
> 25 And he shall speak *great* words against the most High, and shall wear out the saints of the most High, and think to change times and laws: and they shall be given into his hand until a time and times and the dividing of time.

Daniel may or may not have figured the two prophecies were different issues, but they are not the same according to later information through the apostle John: "power was given . . . to continue and given unto him to make war with the saints":

> REVELATION 13
> [5] And there was given unto him a mouth speaking great things and blasphemies; and power was given unto him to continue forty *and* two months.
> [7] And it was given unto him to make war with the saints, and to overcome them: and power was given him over all kindreds, and tongues, and nations.

Power given to the antichrist "to continue" becomes one subject. "Make war with the saints" is another issue. Previously, the antichrist would "wear out the saints". There is a shift from "wear out the saints . . . a time and times and the dividing of time" to an additional "forty and two months . . . to make war with the saints".

Another item to notice is an additional subject (Rev. 13:7) whereby the power is given over "all kindreds, and tongues, and nations", a switch from "wear out the saints" to include "power over all people on earth". What is happening?

The antichrist receives power after Satan has been cast to earth. The antichrist and Satan (the beast with power) will then pursue Satan's war with those having the testimony of Jesus Christ. The "power was given to continue for forty-two months". Evidently the antichrist could not continue without a "power given unto him". This interruption without any power would then be when the antichrist loses any power, when he is "wounded to death", when he is killed!

Scripture does state the antichrist is killed! Unfortunately, various English translations are ambiguous about the terms describing "wounded to death". However, the terms are very specific. The term translated to "wounded" is the root verb for *butcher*.[25] In other uses, the term is translated either "kill" (Rev. 6:4) or "slain" (Rev. 5:6, 9, 12; 6:9; 13:8; 18:24). "Death is separation of soul and body", with a few examples in Matthew 26:59; Mark 10:33; Luke 23:32.[26] The literal meaning is "butchered for separation of soul and body", or "slain to death", or "killed dead"!

The receiving of power will be after the "deadly wound was healed" and when he "did live". This power is an absolute, unrestricted power[27] such as in Luke 12:5, and is a "supra-ordinated power" which comes only from God:[28]

> ROMANS 13
> 1 Let every soul be subject unto the higher powers. For there is no power but of God; the powers that be are ordained of God.

The antichrist is "killed, healed, lives and is given power". With Satan, he is identified as the first beast, who then gives power to another beast, who "exerciseth all power of the first beast".

> REVELATION 13
> 11 And I beheld another beast coming up out of the earth; and he had two horns like a lamb, and he spake as a dragon.
> 12 And he exerciseth all the power of the first beast before him, and causeth the earth and them which dwell therein to worship the first beast, whose deadly wound was healed.
> 13 And he doeth great wonders, so that he maketh fire come down from heaven on the earth in the sight of men,
> 14 And deceiveth them that dwell on the earth by *the means of* those miracles which he had power to do in the sight of the beast; saying to them that dwell on the earth, that they should make an image to the beast, which had the wound by a sword, and did live.
> 15 And he had power to give life unto the image of the beast, that the image of the beast should both speak, and cause that as many as would not worship the image of the beast should be killed.

This second beast is called "another beast", who comes "up out of the earth". Coming up out of the earth probably means someone raised from the dead. The *another* indicates there was someone raised from the dead previously—the antichrist. Remember, the beast with the ten horns comes out of the sea:

> REVELATION 13
> 1 And I stood upon the sand of the sea, and saw a beast rise up out of the sea, having seven heads and ten horns, and upon his horns ten crowns, and upon his heads the name of blasphemy.

The antichrist is not one of those horns. He "came up among them . . . plucked up three of the first horns by the roots . . ." (Dan. 7:8), leaving seven of the original horns (kings) and himself as the eighth king.

The antichrist, who becomes the *first beast* when Satan has control of him, will have come out of the earth as the *other*, whereas the second beast was *another.* The second beast gives "life unto the image of the [first] beast" only "when before the first beast and in the sight of the beast". Satan has to be present for there to be any power so the antichrist can live, and then be within sight of the second beast so he will have power. Then, the second beast can pass on power to the image for life and to speak.

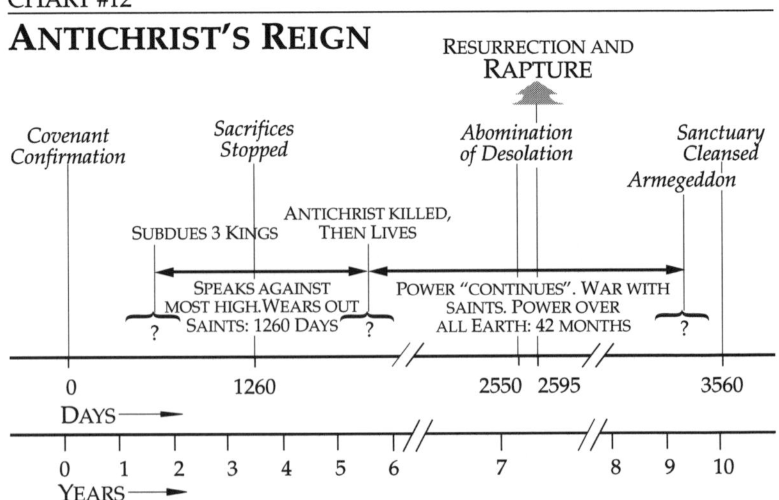

So, after being killed, the antichrist comes alive and will continue for "forty and two months" more. As the beast, he will continue for only forty-two months (1260 days) because GOD allows it to be no longer. (Only GOD can give any power). GOD stops the antichrist at the end of forty-two months—Armageddon. When is this? If this timing were known, then GOD's plan could be identified and the remaining unknown timings determined.

31. First and Second Beasts

The antichrist becomes the first beast when he is healed and lives. The second beast is usually called the *false prophet*. It should be mentioned that today, and in this writing, the term *antichrist* is used rather loosely. Scripture uses the descriptions of "man of sin . . . son of perdition . . . wicked . . . mighty king". The son of perdition—the antichrist—very likely will be the same Judas Iscariot who betrayed Lord Jesus Christ:

> JOHN 17
> [12] While I was with them in the world, I kept them in thy name: those that thou gavest me I have kept, and none of them is lost, but the son of perdition; that the Scripture might be fulfilled.

> II THESSALONIANS 2
> [3] Let no man deceive you by any means: for *that day shall not come,* except there come a falling away first, and that man of sin be revealed, the son of perdition;

During the Last Supper, Jesus Christ did not use the name of Judas Iscariot during His prayer for the disciples. The context is that of those around Him, where "none of them is lost", Judas had already left the Last Supper and would be "the son of perdition . . . the man of sin . . . Wicked . . . mighty king". Also, Lord Jesus Christ identified Judas Iscariot as a devil:

JOHN 6
[70] Jesus answered them, Have not I chosen you twelve, and one of you is a devil?

JOHN 13
[2] And supper being ended, the devil having now put into the heart of Judas Iscariot, Simon's *son,* to betray him;

Both of the two beasts come up out of the earth. Scripture indicates the first beast—the antichrist—is probably Judas Iscariot raised from the dead, killed and then healed.

Who is the second beast? There doesn't appear to be any direct information in Scripture about the identity of the second beast, but there is some circumstantial evidence: it could possibly be Ahithophel.

Ahithophel was a member of King David's council, betrayed him, supported the rebellion of David's son Absalom and then hung himself. Ahithophel and Judas Iscariot had much in common: betrayed their masters for personal gain, supported the opposition and hung themselves—the only two Scripture recordings of self-hanging:

II SAMUEL 17
[23] And when Ahithophel saw that his counsel was not followed, he saddled *his* ass, and arose, and gat him home to his house, to his city, and put his household in order, and hanged himself, and died, and was buried in the sepulchre of his father.

MATTHEW 27
[5] And he cast down the pieces of silver in the temple, and departed, and went and hanged himself.

The story of David, Absalom, and Ahithophel should be studied. The resemblance to the antichrist (by Absalom) and Judas Iscariot (by Ahithophel) are amazing! (II Samuel 13–18:18).

The first beast has control of the military and political systems, whereas the second beast controls the religious system of the whole earth—all under Satan's control. There are some other descriptions for beasts:

REVELATION 17
3 So he carried me away in the spirit into the wilderness:
and I saw a woman sit upon a scarlet-coloured beast, full
of names of blasphemy, having seven heads and ten horns.
5 And upon her forehead *was* a name written, MYSTERY,
BABYLON THE GREAT, THE MOTHER OF HARLOTS AND
ABOMINATIONS OF THE EARTH.
8 The beast that thou sawest was, and is not; and shall
ascend out of the bottomless pit, and go into perdition:
and they that dwell on the earth shall wonder, whose
names were not written in the book of life from the
foundation of the world, when they behold the beast that
was, and is not, and yet is.

A riddle is presented concerning the *seven heads:*

REVELATION 17
10 And there are seven kings: five are fallen, and one is, *and*
the other is not yet come; and when he cometh, he must
continue a short space.
11 And the beast that was, and is not, even he is the eighth
and is of the seven, and goeth into perdition.

It should be realized that the ten horns are those of the beast described by Daniel. These last ten horns represent the kings controlling a military and political system that "make war with the Lamb" (Armageddon):

REVELATION 13
1 And I stood upon the sand of the sea, and saw a beast rise up out of the sea, having seven heads and ten horns, and upon his horns ten crowns, and upon his heads the name of blasphemy.

REVELATION 17
12 And the ten horns which thou sawest are ten kings, which have received no kingdom as yet; but receive power as kings one hour with the beast.

> 14 These shall make war with the Lamb, and the Lamb shall overcome them: for he is Lord of lords, and King of kings: and they that are with him *are* called, and chosen, and faithful.

The seven heads are the kings of Daniel's prophecies. There are eight kings after the antichrist uproots three of ten and he becomes the eighth. This will be fulfilled by the antichrist who "is not yet come and is the eighth and is of the seven".

Daniel's prophecies about the antichrist stop once the antichrist "plants the tabernacles [tent/covering] of his palace—in the glorious mountain"—i.e., dwells in Jerusalem (Dan. 11:45). This is prior to Satan being cast from Heaven and before he (the antichrist) is killed. All this brings up additional evidence that Daniel's third kingdom is involved in "rule of the whole earth" (Dan. 2:39). This third kingdom would precede and then coexist with the fourth kingdom for most of the end time and represent the beast descriptions as given in Revelation. The third kingdom is conquered by the antichrist, and becomes part of the fourth kingdom with these two kingdoms being the seven heads and the ten horns of the beast in Revelation.

The ten horns (kings) represent a military and political system under Satan's control, and the seven heads (kings) represent a religious system also under Satan's direction. These are the ten horns and seven heads that have control over the whole earth. The seven religious leaders are destroyed or removed when the ten kings (military) destroy Babylon and the religious system just prior to Armageddon. One part of the Revelation beast destroying the other part indicates a divided kingdom, also denoted by Daniel's vision of an image with toes of clay and iron (Dan. 2:41).

The beast having seven heads and ten horns represents systems and should not be confused with the "first and second beasts", which represent the individuals controlling these systems.

The riddle about "seven kings: five are fallen, one is and another is not yet come . . . beast . . . was . . . is not . . . is the eighth, and is of the seven" is partially answered in Zechariah 11. In that Chapter, shepherds are described who "slay those in their flocks" and have no pity:

ZECHARIAH 11
4 Thus saith the LORD my God; Feed the flock of the slaughter;
5 Whose possessors slay them, and hold themselves not guilty: and they that sell them say, Blessed *be* the LORD; for I am rich: and their own shepherds pity them not.

Three of these shepherds are cut off:

ZECHARIAH 11
8 Three shepherds also I cut off in one month; and my soul lothed them, and their soul also abhorred me.

This would be three who are fallen, and a fourth could be *Bands*:

ZECHARIAH 11
14 Then I cut asunder mine other staff, *even Bands,* that I might break the brotherhood between Judah and Israel

Although He is, Jesus Christ most certainly cannot be counted among the "seven heads of the MOTHER OF HARLOTS"! But Satan also is.

To recapitulate: of the *five who are fallen,* there are numbers 1, 2, and 3 (Zech. 11:8). *Bands* has fallen (cut asunder) to be counted as number 4. Satan *is* and would be counted as number 6. So identification is needed for one more who has fallen, number 5. Then number 7 and 8 need to be identified.

The antichrist will be number 5. He will fall when he is killed with a deadly wound. "The beast that was and is not" must describe the antichrist who *is not* when he is killed, and then *is* when he "lives by the power" of Satan. This beast is number 8 where "he is the eighth and is of the seven," because both number 5 (the antichrist) and number 6 (Satan) become one upon antichrist's resurrection and both were among the seven.

Number 7 will be the false prophet (second beast), who "came out of the earth" and previously had been fallen. However, he will not be fallen while he is the second beast; he and the antichrist go straight to the lake of fire (Rev. 19:20). Whew! This is explained further in a later section, "Death and Hell".

At this point, it is concluded that the first beast will have control over the horns of the beast out of the sea, and the second beast will control the heads of the beast of Babylon—all under Satan's direction until Armageddon, or very shortly after. These two end-time kingdoms are the same as Daniel's third and fourth kingdoms, which will rule over the whole earth.

The false prophet (second beast) is described as the "idol shepherd", probably meaning the shepherd who will make the image speak:

> ZECHARIAH 11
> [17] Woe to the idol shepherd that leaveth the flock! the sword *shall be* upon his arm, and upon his right eye: his arm shall be clean dried up, and his right eye shall be utterly darkened.

> REVELATION 13
> [15] And he had power to give life unto the image of the beast, that the image of the beast should both speak, and cause that as many as would not worship the image of the beast should be killed.

32. Armageddon

To determine when Armageddon occurs, the analysis must turn to a completely separate, and seemingly unrelated, time prophecy. This time increment is defined in the fifth sounding of an angel, the Fifth Trumpet:

REVELATION 9
[5] And to them it was given that they should not kill them, but that they should be tormented five months: and their torment *was* as the torment of a scorpion, when he striketh a man.

Events of the Fifth Trumpet are for a period of five months (150 days). This trumpet is in the first of three woes and include the Sixth and Seventh Trumpets:

REVELATION 8
[13] And I beheld, and heard an angel flying through the midst of heaven, saying with a loud voice, Woe, woe, woe, to the inhabiters of the earth by reason of the other voices of the trumpet of the three angels, which are yet to sound!

The five months of the Fifth Trumpet to the Sixth Trumpet is reinforced to mean exactly five months, because the Sixth Trumpet includes angels prepared right down to the hour:

REVELATION 9
[14] Saying to the sixth angel which had the trumpet, Loose the four angels which are bound in the great river Euphrates.
[15] And the four angels were loosed, which were prepared for an hour, and a day, and a month, and a year, for to slay the third part of men.

The third woe is the Seventh Trumpet, where Rapture is indicated:

REVELATION 10
[7] But in the days of the voice of the seventh angel, when he shall begin to sound, the mystery of God should be finished, as he hath declared to his servants the prophets.

REVELATION 14
[15] And another angel came out of the temple, crying with a loud voice to him that sat on the cloud, Thrust in thy sickle, and reap: for the time is come for thee to reap; for the

harvest of the earth is ripe.

REVELATION 15
1 And I saw another sign in heaven, great and marvellous,
seven angels having the seven last plagues; for in them is
filled up the wrath of God.
2 And I saw as it were a sea of glass mingled with fire: and
them that had gotten the victory over the beast, and over
his image, and over his mark, *and* over the number of his
name, stand on the sea of glass, having the harps of God.

The Seventh Trumpet starts at day 2595 after covenant confirmation.

The length of time for the Fifth Trumpet has been preordained to be five months. The timing of the Sixth Trumpet has also been preordained. And (presumably) the duration of the Seventh Trumpet has been preordained. The Seventh Trumpet ends with Armageddon:

REVELATION 16
13 And I saw three unclean spirits like frogs *come* out of the
mouth of the dragon, and out of the mouth of the beast,
and out of the mouth of the false prophet.
14 For they are the spirits of devils, working miracles, *which*
go forth unto the kings of the earth and of the whole world,
to gather them to the battle of that great day of God
Almighty.
16 And he gathered them together into a place called in the
Hebrew tongue Armageddon.

REVELATION 19
19 And I saw the beast, and the kings of the earth, and their
armies, gathered together to make war against him that
sat on the horse, and against his army.

Are the time periods for each of the three woes going to be five months each? Apparently. Showing this to be the case is one of the intents for describing the woes and emphasizing the hour, day, month, and year. With reasonable assurance, the Sixth and Seventh Trumpets are considered to have time increments of five months each. If this is the case, then Armageddon occurs at 2595 days plus 150 days (five months) and is 2745 days from covenant confirmation.

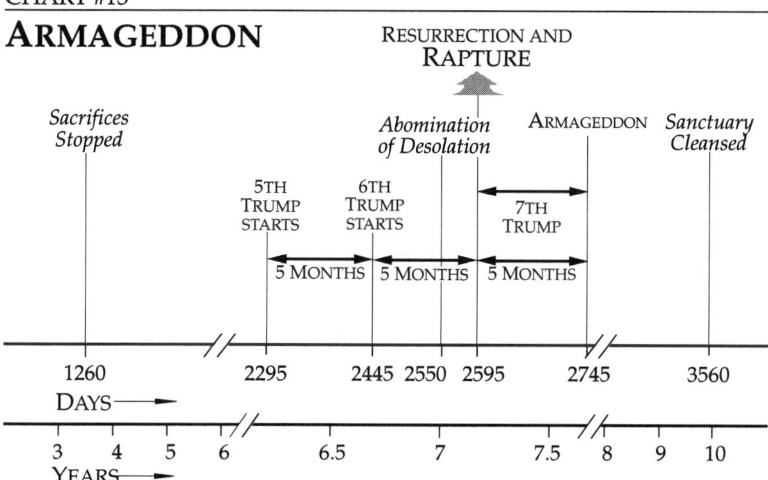

33. Antichrist Gets Ready

Daniel also provided a prophecy about "a time": very likely a period of one year. The year starts after the antichrist will "pluck three kings, stand up . . . overflow kingdom . . . break prince of covenant and make league with him and become strong" (Dan. 7:8; 11:3, 21–23). Then, the antichrist distributes prey, spoil and riches to gain support from his following and "he shall forecast his devises against the strongholds". He does this for one year—a time:

DANIEL 11

23 And after the league *made* with him he shall work deceitfully: for he shall come up, and shall become strong with a small people.

> [24] He shall enter peaceably even upon the fattest places of the province; and he shall do *that* which his fathers have not done, nor his fathers' fathers; he shall scatter among them the prey, and spoil, and riches: *yea,* and he shall forecast his devices against the strong holds, even for a time.

The forecast *devices* means to "plot" or "contrive" his political and military plans. This will be very soon after obtaining the kingdom by flatteries or intrigue, and making a league with the prince of the covenant. Probably, this league is to allow continuation of sacrifices based on some sort of bribery or false agreements for mutual support.

As a side issue, the "prey" that the antichrist will provide to his followers just happens to be female captives, the choicest pickings. The term used is *female,* and a description is given (see also Esther 9:15):

> ESTHER 8
> [11] Wherein the king granted the Jews which *were* in every city to gather themselves together, and to stand for their life, to destroy, to slay, and to cause to perish, all the power of the people and province that would assault them, *both* little ones and women, and *to take* the spoil of them for a prey,

> DANIEL 11
> [37] Neither shall he regard the God of his fathers, nor the desire of women, nor regard any god: for he shall magnify himself above all.

The antichrist's actions of "neither . . . regard . . . the desire of women" becomes quite clear! And he won't care about the desires of anyone!

34. Outer Court

The apostle John was told not to measure the court around the temple, because it will be trampled for forty-two months:

REVELATION 11
[2] But the court which is without the temple leave out, and measure it not; for it is given unto the Gentiles: and the holy city shall they tread under foot forty *and* two months.

Trampling would be expected to end at the completion of GOD's Wrath, at 2745 days after covenant confirmation. This *trampling* is the same length of time and same type of wording for "power continue" when the antichrist is over all "kindreds, and tongues, and nations". The *power* ends at Armageddon, and *trampling* should end at the same time.

35. Hour and Day Prophecies

Completely different types of time prophecies occur when they are identified by "one hour" and "about . . . half an hour":

REVELATION 8
[1] And when he had opened the seventh seal, there was silence in heaven about the space of half an hour.

REVELATION 17
[12] And the ten horns which thou sawest are ten kings, which have received no kingdom as yet; but receive power as kings one hour with the beast.
[13] These have one mind, and shall give their power and strength unto the beast.
[14] These shall make war with the Lamb, and the Lamb shall overcome them: for he is Lord of lords, and King of kings: and they that are with him *are* called, and chosen, and faithful.
[16] And the ten horns which thou sawest upon the beast, these shall hate the whore, and shall make her desolate and naked, and shall eat her flesh, and burn her with fire.

Where one week is equivalent to seven years, as in the case of the seventy weeks determined upon Israel, then there should be a relationship where one week is seven years, one day becomes one year, and one hour becomes fifteen days (one twenty-fourth of 360 days). In the case of "silence in heaven about the space of half an hour", the time would be seven and one-half days. The word *about* indicates an approximation with the meaning probably being "seven days".

The "ten kings . . . receive power . . . one hour" would be those gathered for Armageddon. From the time they start to gather to fight Lord Jesus Christ and until Armageddon is all over there would be fifteen days. Fifteen days does not seem very long to collect armies from around the entire world, but they will have some supernatural capabilities:

> ISAIAH 5
> 26 And he will lift up an ensign to the nations from far, and will hiss unto them from the end of the earth: and, behold, they shall come with speed swiftly:
> 27 None shall be weary nor stumble among them; none shall slumber nor sleep; neither shall the girdle of their loins be loosed, nor the latchet of their shoes be broken:

> JOEL 2
> 1 Blow ye the trumpet in Zion, and sound an alarm in my holy mountain: let all the inhabitants of the land tremble: for the day of the LORD cometh, for *it is* nigh at hand;
> 7 They shall run like mighty men; they shall climb the wall like men of war; and they shall march every one on his ways, and they shall not break their ranks:
> 8 Neither shall one thrust another; they shall walk every one in his path: and *when* they fall upon the sword, they shall not be wounded.

In addition, the fifteen days (one hour) to collect for Armageddon will include the destruction of Babylon by the ten kings:

> REVELATION 17
> 16 And the ten horns which thou sawest upon the beast, these shall hate the whore, and shall make her desolate and naked, and shall eat her flesh, and burn her with fire.

REVELATION 18
[10] Standing afar off for the fear of her torment, saying, Alas,
alas, that great city Babylon, that mighty city! for in one
hour is thy judgment come.
[17] For in one hour so great riches is come to nought. And
every shipmaster, and all the company in ships, and sailors,
and as many as trade by sea, stood afar off,
[19] And they cast dust on their heads, and cried, weeping
and wailing, saying, Alas, alas, that great city, wherein were
made rich all that had ships in the sea by reason of her
costliness! for in one hour is she made desolate.

There is a Scripture statement about all of Babylon's plagues coming in "one day", and this is different than the previous three quotations of "one hour". However, the one-day prophecy defines the time as "plagues, death, mourning, famine, fire and judgment", whereas the one-hour prophecies are directed only to mourning, as indicated by "alas, alas, cried, weeping and wailing":

REVELATION 18
[8] Therefore shall her plagues come in one day, death, and
mourning, and famine; and she shall be utterly burned
with fire: for strong *is* the Lord God who judgeth her.

Apparently the use of *one day* does, indeed, refer to a literal one day, an evening and a morning, and indicates swiftness of destruction. The three statements of *one hour* would be an emphasis upon mourning and represent a fifteen-day time increment.

Evidently, nonbelievers finally realize their situation is hopeless, but they will still prepare to fight GOD at Armageddon as a last attempt of pride and self-sufficiency!

36. Church in Smyrna

Yet another time prophecy fits into end times where *ten days* is used for the church in Smyrna:

REVELATION 2
10 Fear none of those things which thou shalt suffer: behold, the devil shall cast *some* of you into prison, that ye may be tried; and ye shall have tribulation ten days: be thou faithful unto death, and I will give thee a crown of life.
11 He that hath an ear, let him hear what the Spirit saith unto the churches; He that overcometh shall not be hurt of the second death.

Surprise! Another reminder: the church letters are for all churches and for each individual!

Here is an indication that the Tribulation will start ten years (for Believers) prior to the Rapture—965 days before the covenant confirmation. This would be two years, eight months and five days earlier (when counting with 360-day years) than covenant confirmation.

According to history, Smyrna suffered ten persecutions between A.D. 64 and A.D. 313, ten years of persecution under Diocletian from A.D. 303 to A.D. 313, and was destroyed and rebuilt ten times.[29] These may well be foreshadows of the end times.

Scripture seems to be stating there will be Tribulation for Believers before the programs start for Israel and for nonbelievers:

I PETER 2
21 For even hereunto were ye called; because Christ also suffered for us, leaving us an example, that ye should follow his steps:

I PETER 4
17 For the time *is come* that judgment must begin at the house of God: and if *it* first *begin* at us, what shall the end *be* of them that obey not the gospel of God?

The situation boils down to believing a popular concept (tradition of the past 150 years) of only a seven-year Tribulation without Believers being present, or to believe the letters to His churches. The letter to Smyrna indicates "tribulation ten days", which could be ten years. Truth will be known whenever the events occur!

37. Summary: Events and Times

Chart 14 summarizes most of the event times and activity time periods discussed. Some potential modifications are mentioned as follows:

- *Silence in* Heaven. Likely to be *seven days* after the Seventh Seal is opened—is not shown.
- *Fifteen days* for collecting armies for Armageddon seems reasonable as well as for including the destruction of Babylon. However, the destruction period may be a shorter time interval and is not shown. Nor is a mourning period shown.
- The *ten days* (ten 360-day years) of Tribulation for Believers is only implied. It's not expected to be less than 2595 days (7.2 years). It will probably be the longer period, but a start day may not even be noticed; there has been tribulation since the Crucifixion!
- Some time interval should be needed for the antichrist to "uproot three kings and make a league with the prince of the covenant", but this has not been determined nor included.
- The date (day number) for Armageddon should be correct. However, the other time intervals determined from that time (2745 days) may not be accurate. Armageddon should represent the completion of GOD's Wrath on man. However, Lord Jesus Christ may use another twenty-one days for complete control of Satan and his demons:

DANIEL 10
[13] But the prince of the kingdom of Persia withstood me one and twenty days: but, lo,

CHART #14

Summary: Events and Times

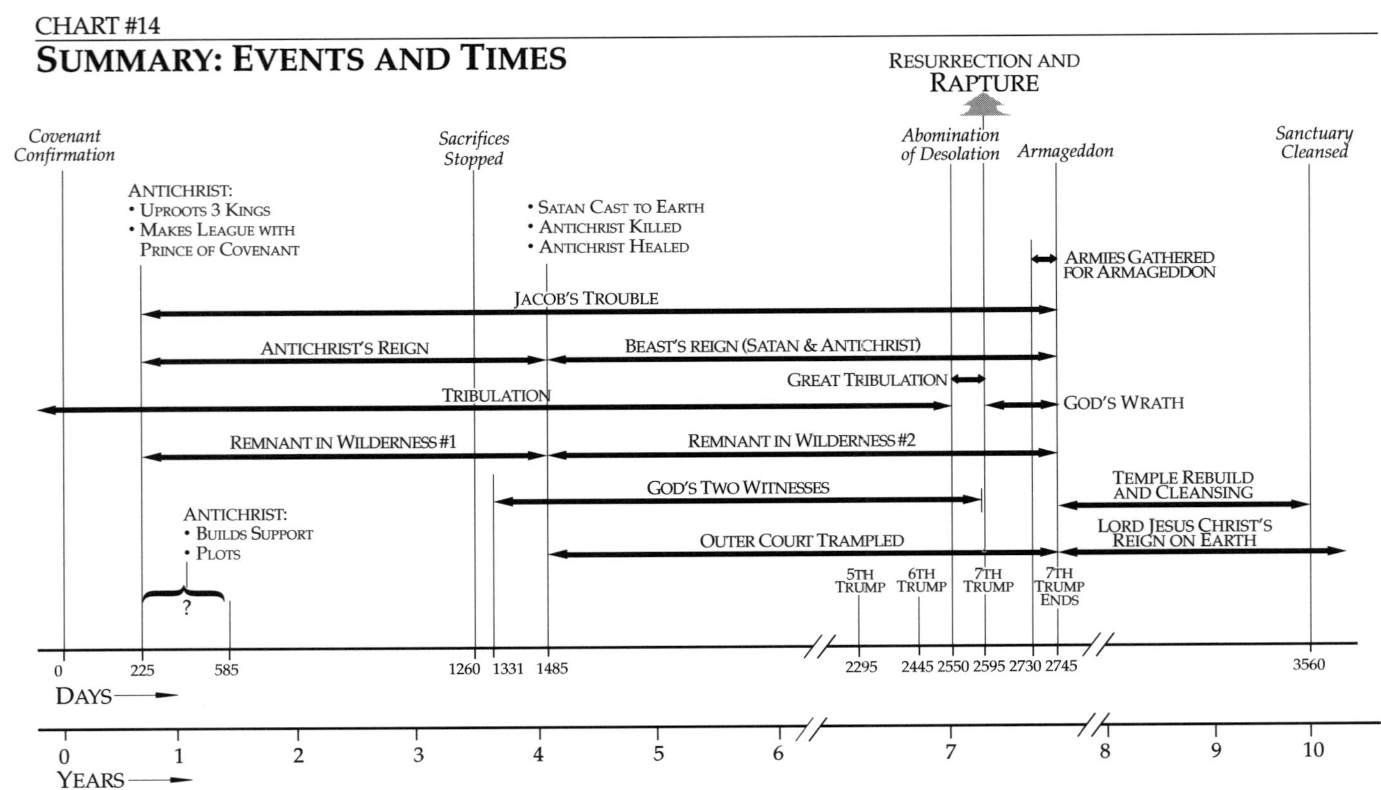

> Michael, one of the chief princes, came to help me; and I remained there with the kings of Persia.

This would mean that the time intervals for Jacob's Trouble, the antichrist's reign, the beast's reign, and Israel's remnant in the wildernesses are to end twenty-one days after Armageddon. Satan will continue his attempt to annihilate Israel right up to the bitter end.

- Another factor, which could require minor modifications, would be if the antichrist remained dead for three days before being healed. This is not known—only problematical—and the three days are not added into the overall timing.

The summary chart is intended to be more accurate than previous attempts, not necessarily finalized.

Chapter Seven

38. The Covenant

All the time periods which have been identified are related to *confirm the covenant* (Dan. 9:27). Daniel gave no details about the *covenant* nor did he provide much information concerning how it would be confirmed. However, some information is available through other prophets—primarily Isaiah. Isaiah described a *covenant which is with death and with hell* and called it an *agreement:*

> ISAIAH 28
> [15] Because ye have said, We have made a covenant with death, and with hell are we at agreement; when the overflowing scourge shall pass through, it shall not come unto us: for we have made lies our refuge, and under falsehood have we hid ourselves:
> [18] And your covenant with death shall be disannulled, and your agreement with hell shall not stand; when the overflowing scourge shall pass through, then ye shall be trodden down by it.

Isaiah proceeds to indicate "a consumption upon the whole earth". The term translated to *consumption* refers to "completion, consummation, utter end, destruction".[30] The "covenant with death and with hell" will be a key issue during the end times and GOD's Wrath:

> ISAIAH 28
> [21] For the *LORD* shall rise up as *in* mount Perazim, he shall be wroth as *in* the valley of Gibeon, that he may do his work, his strange work; and bring to pass his act, his strange act.

> [22] Now therefore be ye not mockers, lest your bands be made strong: for I have heard from the Lord GOD of hosts a consumption, even determined upon the whole earth.

The phrase about God's Wrath "as in the valley of Gibeon" relates to historical events about a deceitful agreement, disobedience to GOD's commands, the sun standing still and destruction of an army with hailstones (Joshua 9–10). These are indicative of end-times intent.

Five of Isaiah's prophecies include details of the "covenant with death and with hell." They all relate to end times and Wrath of GOD. Although primarily directed to Israel, they are to the whole world. A summary list of Isaiah's prophecies indicating end times, GOD's Wrath and (subsequent) real peace is Isaiah 8:9; 10:6–7, 17, 23; 11:11–12; 12:1–6; 13:6, 9, 11, 13; 14:7, 12, 22, 25; 16:5; 18:3; 19:2, 19.

History has foreshadowed some of these events, mainly the destruction of Jerusalem and Israel prior to the exile to Babylon. Many of these prophecies were given at the time when Ahaz was king of Judah and they were also directed to him. Ahaz is a prime example of making a covenant with death and with hell. When Rezin of Damascus and Pekah of (North) Israel attacked Ahaz (Judah), Ahaz held them off. But he then turned to Assyria (Isa. 7:1; II Kings 6:5–8) for help in return for his submission to Assyria and payment of the temple treasures. Ahaz had been told by the Lord he would be kept safe, but he would not trust GOD (Isa. 7:4, 10–12). The results were additional wars but with Edom and the Philistines (II Chron. 28:17–18) and also with Ahaz's so-called protector: Assyria (II Chron. 28:20).

In addition to his not trusting the Lord, Ahaz "worshipped gods of Assyria" (II Chron. 28:23), "worshipped other gods in high places" (II Chron. 28:25; II Kings 16:4), "passed his son through fire" (II Kings 16:3), and "made images" (II Chron. 28:2).

Basically, the essence of the covenant with death and with hell has four main features:

1. Not relying on God
2. Relying on others for protection
3. Paying for the protection
4. Worshipping other gods or worshipping in wrong places, in wrong ways and with the wrong attitude

The symptoms of this *covenant* involve "refuge in lies, falsehood, scorn, mockery, pride, hypocrisy, evildoers, folly, wickedness, unrighteous decrees, take away right, robbery, people against one another, idols, charmers, wizards, confusion, no justice, no truth, vanity, mischief, iniquity, violence, shedding innocent blood and (far from least) no faith nor trust in God" (Isa. 8; 9–10; 59).

It appears very likely that "confirm the covenant" will fit the category of a covenant with death and with hell. The league between the antichrist and the prince of the covenant should be another agreement of the same nature.

During the reign of the beast at end times, the covenant with death and with hell will also be represented as the mark of the beast:

> Revelation 13
> [16] And he causeth all, both small and great, rich and poor, free and bond, to receive a mark in their right hand, or in their foreheads:
> [17] And that no man might buy or sell, save he that had the mark, or the name of the beast, or the number of his name.

> Revelation 14
> [9] And the third angel followed them, saying with a loud voice, If any man worship the beast and his image, and receive *his* mark in his forehead, or in his hand,
> [10] The same shall drink of the wine of the wrath of God which is poured out without mixture into the cup of his indignation; and he shall be tormented with fire and brimstone in the presence of the holy angels, and in the presence of the Lamb:

Evidently, there will be three types of such covenants with death and with hell:

1. Nations
2. Religions
3. Individuals

39. Death and Hell

The covenant with death and with hell has been described in other ways:

> ISAIAH 9
> 14 Therefore the LORD will cut off from Israel head and tail, branch and rush, in one day.

> ISAIAH 9
> 15 The ancient and honourable, he *is* the head; and the prophet that teacheth lies, he *is* the tail.

> ISAIAH 19
> 15 Neither shall there be *any* work for Egypt, which the head or tail, branch or rush, may do.

The clearest definitions appear where "ancient . . . honorable . . . head" is related to death, and the "prophet that teacheth lies, he is the tail" relates to hell.

These prophecies and the previous ones about death and hell need many terms defined. Here they will be summarized only.

- *Death* is often an actual personification of death.
- *Head* refers to chief or leader.
- *Ancient* is old or grown old.
- *Honorable* means to lift up. In conjunction with *head,* it has a meaning of self-appointed.[31]
- The term translated to *branch* is used only one other time in Scripture, as a "wicked man" (Job 15:20, 32).

Therefore, the head can be concluded to be Satan!

- The *tail* is a prophet *"teaching lies . . . pleasing words which are a sham and deceitful"*.[32] The tail will be *"out of the serpent's root"* (Isa. 14:29) and out of the earth (swamp), where *rush* indicates a bent head—a snake or serpent. This is the false prophet, probably raised from the dead.

So, the covenant with death and hell is made, symbolically, through a serpent—a snake—where the head is Satan, the body is the antichrist making agreements (league) related to politics and war, and the tail is the false prophet who has no power unless "attached" to (within view of) the head. The religious and "mark of the beast" covenants are through the tail. Satan is the head controlling the antichrist and false prophet. This will occur after Satan is cast to earth.

Another point determined through Old Testament terms is the head of the serpent is the "first death". The first death was accomplished through Adam and Eve (physical death) and is through the antichrist by war. The "second death" is accomplished through the tail and mark of the beast.

The Fourth Seal opened by Lord Jesus Christ includes Death and Hell:

> REVELATION 6
> 7 And when he had opened the fourth seal, I heard the voice of the fourth beast say, Come and see.
> 8 And I looked, and behold a pale horse: and his name that sat on him was Death, and Hell followed with him. And power was given unto them over the fourth part of the earth, to kill with sword, and with hunger, and with death, and with the beasts of the earth.

The lake of fire and brimstone is defined as death and hell—the second death:

> REVELATION 20
> 14 And death and hell were cast into the lake of fire. This is

> the second death.
> 15 And whosoever was not found written in the book of life was cast into the lake of fire.
>
> REVELATION 21
> 8 But the fearful, and unbelieving, and the abominable, and murderers, and whoremongers, and sorcerers, and idolaters, and all liars, shall have their part in the lake which burneth with fire and brimstone: which is the second death.

Various forms of the covenant with death and with hell have been around for a long, long time!

In whatever form it may be, enough emphasis cannot be placed on the meanings of the covenant with death and with hell—meanings to nations, religions, and individuals—now, later or end times!

40. Antichrist and Covenant

Isaiah used different descriptions to show the antichrist will not confirm the covenant and the antichrist will not be a direct participant in "covenant with [second] death and with hell" until he has been killed and lives. Isaiah used the symbolism of trees to compare the antichrist to Israel:

> ISAIAH 9
> 9 And all the people shall know, *even* Ephraim and the inhabitant of Samaria, that say in the pride and stoutness of heart,
> 10 The bricks are fallen down, but we will build with hewn stones: the sycomores are cut down, but we will change *them into* cedars.

Ephraim is a tribe of Israel, but in general is considered to be most of the northern portion and is often a name used to describe all of Israel. Ephraim, Samaria and Israel are sometimes combined as one because there has been a lack of definitive boundaries and, in the past, there has been common idol worship:

> II CHRONICLES 25
> [7] But there came a man of God to him, saying, 0 king, let not the army of Israel go with thee; for the LORD *is* not with Israel, *to wit, with* all the children of Ephraim.
>
> ISAIAH 7
> [2] And it was told the house of David, saying, Syria is confederate with Ephraim. And his heart was moved, and the heart of his people, as the trees of the wood are moved with the wind.

These people have "pride and stoutness of heart". Their inner nature is pride. The bricks relate to pride where the first usage related in Scripture describes the Tower of Babel, which symbolizes "pride, stubbornness, rebellion and man's folly":

> GENESIS 11
> [3] And they said one to another, Go to, let us make brick and burn them throughly. And they had brick for stone, and slime had they for morter.
> [4] And they said, Go to, let us build us a city and a tower, whose top *may* reach unto heaven; and let us make us a name, lest we be scattered abroad upon the face of the whole earth.

The sycamore tree is a type of fig tree, but the fruit is a nuisance to harvest and not as desirable as normal figs. This could represent a rebellious, stubborn Israel. Ephraim would (then) represent a proud, idol worshipping Israel and Samaria.

Bricks, especially early ones made of sun-dried mud, should represent no pride in themselves. However, hewn stones are not to be used for an altar, if shaped by a tool, they are considered as idol worship:

Exodus 20
[25] And if thou wilt make me an altar of stone, thou shalt not build it of hewn stone: for if thou lift up thy tool upon it, thou hast polluted it.

Cedar must represent the antichrist. If the sycamore represents an errant and unbelieving Israel, then God will punish Israel with a cedar:

Ezekiel 31
[3] Behold, the Assyrian *was* a cedar in Lebanon with fair branches, and with a shadowing shroud, and of an high stature; and his top was among the thick boughs.
[9] I have made him fair by the multitude of his branches; so that all the trees of Eden, that *were* in the garden of God, envied him.
[10] Therefore thus saith the Lord God; Because thou hast lifted up thyself in height, and he hath shot up his top among the thick boughs, and his heart is lifted up in his height;
[11] I have therefore delivered him into the hand of the mighty one of the heathen; he shall surely deal with him: I have driven him out for his wickedness.

Note: Assyria and the antichrist are the same:

Isaiah 10
[5] 0 Assyrian. the rod of mine anger, and the staff in their hand is mine indignation.
[24] Therefore thus saith the Lord God of hosts, 0 my people that dwellest in Zion, be not afraid of the Assyrian: he shall smite thee with a rod, and shall lift up his staff against thee, after the manner of Egypt.

Isaiah 14
[25] That I will break the Assyrian in my land, and upon my mountains tread him under foot: then shall his yoke depart from off them, and his burden depart from off their shoulders.

Although the format used to describe an errant Israel being cut down and under a cedar is similar to the format for covenant with death and with hell, the descriptions are different. The format indicates a relationship, but they are still different. The antichrist, prior to being killed and lives is not a direct part of the serpent of death and hell.

The antichrist does not confirm the covenant, but Satan does through "the people of the prince that shall come"—Satan being that prince (Dan. 9:26).

Lord Jesus Christ has instructed to watch! This could include to watch for various treaties, agreements, leagues, and covenants between nations and religious groups, and then watch for the essence and symptoms of the covenant with death and with hell!

It should be noted that the covenant with death and with hell has been treated as one (in this writing). However, the wording is "a covenant with death . . . and with hell at agreement" (Isa. 28:15, 18). This could mean a covenant and an agreement, one with death and one with hell. These would be different but also would be related. No attempt has been made to separate them. The best conclusion is still to *watch!*

Chapter Eight

41. The United States of America

A question is often brought up about whether the United States is mentioned in Scripture. It could be the nation described in Isaiah 18.[33] Note that it could be. A definite case is attempted to show the United States, but confirmation must await the unfolding of end-time events.

> Isaiah 18
> [1] Woe to the land shadowing with wings, which *is* beyond the rivers of Ethiopia:

The first word, *Woe,* warns this nation of great sorrow, grief, misery, and trouble to come. The "shadowing with wings" could be the national emblem of the United States: an eagle with spread wings. It is also symbolic of protection by God, which has been the case for all history of the United States:

> Psalm 17
> [8] Keep me as the apple of the eye; hide me under the shadow of thy wings,

> Psalm 36
> [7] How excellent *is* thy lovingkindness, O God! therefore the children of men put their trust under the shadow of thy wings.

The *wings* can have an additional meaning, a reference to extremities of land or earth, "a land at an extreme . . . ends of the earth or corners of the earth".[34] The *land* is beyond and at an extremity of the earth from Israel. Where is the land "beyond the rivers of Ethiopia"? To find this land at an extremity, or long distance away, a simple experiment is suggested. Using a length of string and a globe of the earth, place one end of the string on Jerusalem and swing the string across Ethiopia and around the globe, making a "great circle". The "land . . . beyond" seems to be the United States, a land at an extremity of the earth in relation to Israel!

The Ethiopia of today is not the same Ethiopia as when Isaiah wrote the words. Were the words intended to mean the Ethiopia in existence when the prophecy would be fulfilled? Probably. In Scripture, *Ethiopia* meant a variety of locations, such as Nubia or Sudan (south of Egypt), a part of the West Arabian peninsula, area of Yemen or modern Aswan.

The string going across the Ethiopia of today would also go across areas approximating the average location of Old-Testament Ethiopia. The "land . . . beyond" would still be the United States.

> ISAIAH 18
> 2 That sendeth ambassadors by the sea, even in vessels of bulrushes upon the waters, *saying*, Go, ye swift messengers, to a nation scattered and peeled, to a people terrible from their beginning hitherto; a nation meted out and trodden down, whose land the rivers have spoiled!

The United States has many ambassadors—probably more than other nations. However, the term Isaiah used for *ambassadors* has a primary use of *spying* or *convincing* to make war during the end times:

> JOSHUA 9
> 4 They did work wilily, and went and made as if they had been ambassadors, and took old sacks upon their asses, and wine bottles, old, and rent, and bound up;

> JEREMIAH 49
> 14 I have heard a rumour from the LORD, and an ambassador

is sent unto the heathen, *saying*, Gather ye together, and come against her, and rise up to the battle.

OBADIAH 1
[1] The vision of Obadiah. Thus saith the Lord GOD concerning Edom; We have heard a rumour from the LORD, and an ambassador is sent among the heathen, Arise ye, and let us rise up against her in battle.

The "bulrushes" are porous paper, and vessels are receptacles. The meaning is difficult to figure out unless it is a satirical statement about a lot of government paper, and it goes around to other nations—paper money sure does!

The *messengers* appear to be those from GOD (angels or people):

HAGGAI 1
[13] Then spake Haggai the LORD's messenger in the LORD's message unto the people, saying, I *am* with you, saith the LORD.

MALACHI 2
[7] For the priest's lips should keep knowledge, and they should seek the law at his mouth: for he *is* the messenger of the LORD of hosts.

MALACHI 3
[1] Behold, I will send my messenger, and he shall prepare the way before me: and the Lord, whom ye seek, shall suddenly come to his temple, even the messenger of the covenant, whom ye delight in: behold, he shall come, saith the LORD of hosts.

A "nation scattered and peeled" could describe a nation widespread and large, or maybe a nation made up of peoples scattered to it from other parts of the world. Also, United States citizens are scattered throughout the world as tourists and business representatives. The term for *peeled* usually means "independent" or "obstinate" and could be a description for the United States.[35]

The term for *terrible* has two meanings.[36] It can mean "to be feared" or "reverence for GOD":

ISAIAH 21
[1] The burden of the desert of the sea. As whirlwinds in the south pass through; *so* it cometh from the desert, from a terrible land.

II CHRONICLES 6
[31] That they may fear thee, to walk in thy ways, so long as they live in the land which thou gavest unto our fathers.

The United States has been "terrible" as a superpower in recent history and also "terrible"—same term as *fear* (*rever*ence)—from the beginning based on the nation's founding in awe and respect for GOD.

A nation "meted out" is literally one that has been *line line out*, or surveyed extensively. Although not exclusive to the United States, its surveying has been very extensive.

The "land the rivers have spoiled!" is difficult to understand. Isaiah is the only writer of Scripture who used the term for *spoiled*—in this Chapter only—and he used other terms to indicate *spoil* with the meaning of "destroy". His term probably is a root word for *cleave*.[37] The river systems in the United States are relatively unique compared to most countries, and very few rivers flow across other national boundaries. The river systems do "cleave" (slice) through the country in many areas.

ISAIAH 18
[3] All ye inhabitants of the world, and dwellers on the earth, see ye when he lifteth up an ensign on the mountains; and when he bloweth a trumpet, hear ye.

Twice, the "inhabitants of the world" are instructed to pay attention; something "he" does will have great significance. The world is to "see ye, when he lifteth up an ensign on the mountains". Is this a reference to a national emblem of an eagle with spread wings? Where are the mountains? The ensign could be the national emblem on top of a flagpole. The mountains should be considered from Isaiah's viewpoint, namely in Israel, and Mount Zion is mentioned at the end of the prophecy.

The second notice is "hear yea" in reference to when "he bloweth a trumpet". It is likely that verse 3 is to establish a time frame for what is to follow, and when the woe occurs. The ensign and "bloweth a trumpet" may be used to describe the Day of the Lord:

> ZECHARIAH 9
> 14 And the LORD shall be seen over them, and his arrow shall go forth as the lightning: and the Lord GOD shall blow the trumpet, and shall go with whirlwinds of the south.
> 16 And the LORD their God shall save them in that day as the flock of his people: for they *shall be as* the stones of a crown, lifted up as an ensign upon his land.

The subject is now changed, without doubt, to the Lord and His actions:

> ISAIAH 18
> 4 For so the LORD said unto me, I will take my rest, and I will consider in my dwelling place like a clear heat upon herbs, *and* like a cloud of dew in the heat of harvest.

The Lord will "rest": kind of sit back and watch. The nation's punishment is a sure thing, but its extent may not be totally enumerated. The term used for *rest* means "rest . . . rest, repose, have quiet, be undisturbed".[38] Is this *rest* the *silence* after opening the Seventh Seal?

> REVELATION 8
> 1 And when he had opened the seventh seal, there was silence in heaven about the space of half an hour.

The punishment will not be a light one. A "clear heat upon herbs" is like the hot sun on crops requiring moisture, or they will wither. A "cloud of dew in the heat of harvest" will ruin a crop by molding.

Sometime prior to the harvest (Rapture), the nation will have its "sprigs cut off and branches cut down":

> ISAIAH 18
> [5] For afore the harvest, when the bud is perfect, and the
> sour grape is ripening in the flower, he shall both cut off
> the sprigs with pruning hooks, and take away *and* cut down
> the branches.

The timing of *woe* becomes more apparent because it is before the harvest. This harvest is "when the bud is perfect" and ties in with the harvest (and Rapture) in:

> REVELATION 14
> [15] And another angel came out of the temple, crying with a loud voice to him that sat on the cloud, Thrust in thy sickle, and reap: for the time is come for thee to reap; for the harvest of the earth is ripe.
> [16] And he that sat on the cloud thrust in his sickle on the earth; and the earth was reaped.

This harvest (Rapture) is when "the bud is perfect and the earth is ripe for harvest", but during the time while "the sour grape is ripening". The Rapture would be prior to the Wrath of GOD, which later "gathers the sour grapes which are fully ripe":

> REVELATION 14
> [18] And another angel came out from the altar, which had power over fire; and cried with a loud cry to him that had the sharp sickle, saying, Thrust in thy sharp sickle, and gather the clusters of the vine of the earth; for her grapes are fully ripe.
> [19] And the angel thrust in his sickle into the earth, and gathered the vine of the earth, and cast *it* into the great wine-press of the wrath of God.

> ISAIAH 18
> [6] They shall be left together unto the fowls of the mountains,

and to the beasts of the earth: and the fowls shall summer upon them, and all the beasts of the earth shall winter upon them.

Very descriptive! **However, this nation will survive, will repent and will honor the Lord!**

ISAIAH 18
[7] In that time shall the present be brought unto the LORD of hosts of a people scattered and peeled, and from a people terrible from their beginning hitherto; a nation meted out and trodden under foot, whose land the rivers have spoiled, to the place of the name of the Lord of hosts, the mount Zion.

The "present to be taken" to the Lord is an offering:

ZEPHANIAH 3
[10] From beyond the rivers of Ethiopia my suppliants, *even* the daughter of my dispersed, shall bring mine offering.

The "bad news and the good news" about this nation in Isaiah 18 are that it will be severely punished, but it will honor the Lord. (See also Isa. 5:26–29; 14:32; 21:1).

42. Before the Covenant

Some major events are required before the covenant is confirmed, before the world accepts the idea of Israel having festivals, ceremonies and sacrifices. These events are likely to be associated with major wars, especially around Israel, where the surrounding territories are severely damaged but Israel is miraculously protected. Such events may be described in Ezekiel 38–39.

EZEKIEL 38
[2] Son of man, set thy face against Gog, the land of Magog, the chief prince of Meshech and Tubal, and prophesy against him.

3 And say, Thus saith the Lord GOD; Behold, I *am* against
thee, 0 Gog, the chief prince of Meshech and Tubal:
4 And I will turn thee back, and put hooks into thy jaws,
and I will bring thee forth, and all thine army, horses and
horsemen, all of them clothed with all sorts *of armour, even*
a great company *with* bucklers and shields, all of them
handling swords:
5 Persia, Ethiopia, and Libya with them; all of them with
shield and helmet:
6 Gomer, and all his bands; the house of Togarmah of the
north quarters, and all his bands: *and* many people with
thee.
13 Sheba, and Dedan, and the merchants of Tarshish, with
all the young lions thereof, shall say unto thee, Art thou
come to take a spoil? hast thou gathered thy company to
take a prey? to carry away silver and gold, to take away
cattle and goods, to take a great spoil?

There are various thoughts concerning which countries are represented in these prophecies: however, most are probably adjacent to, or relatively close, to Israel. Ezekiel's Gog and Magog are not likely to be the Gog and Magog in Revelation, when "gathering" is after Lord Jesus Christ's "thousand year reign". In Revelation, they are defined as "in the four quarters of the earth", and destruction is by "fire" (only):

REVELATION 20
7 And when the thousand years are expired, Satan shall be
loosed out of his prison,
8 And shall go out to deceive the nations which are in the
four quarters of the earth, Gog and Magog, to gather them
together to battle: the number of whom *is* as the sand of
the sea.
9 And they went up on the breadth of the earth, and
compassed the camp of the saints about, and the beloved
city: and fire came down from God out of heaven, and
devoured them.

The nations identified by Ezekiel attack Israel, and though destroyed by God, the destruction is not necessarily by fire (only) as after the thousand years:

> Ezekiel 38
> [15] And thou shalt come from thy place out of the north parts, thou, and many people with thee, all of them riding upon horses, a great company, and a mighty army:
> [18] And it shall come to pass at the same time when Gog shall come against the land of Israel, saith the Lord God, *that* my fury shall come up in my face.
> [21] And I will call for a sword against him throughout all my mountains, saith the Lord God: every man's sword shall be against his brother.
> [22] And I will plead against him with pestilence and with blood; and I will rain upon him, and upon his bands, and upon the many people that *are* with him, an overflowing *rain*, and great hailstones, fire, and brimstone.
>
> Ezekiel 39
> [2] And I will turn thee back, and leave but the sixth part of thee, and will cause thee to come up from the north parts, and will bring thee upon the mountains of Israel:
> [3] And I will smite thy bow out of thy left hand, and will cause thine arrows to fall out of thy right hand.
> [4] Thou shalt fall upon the mountains of Israel, thou, and all thy bands, and the people that *is* with thee: I will give thee unto the ravenous birds of every sort, and *to* the beasts of the field to be devoured.
> [5] Thou shalt fall upon the open field: for I have spoken *it*, saith the Lord God.
> [6] And I will send a fire on Magog, and among them that dwell carelessly in the isles: and they shall know that I *am* the Lord.

It should be noted that the events in Ezekiel 38–39 are not Armageddon, nor in the judgment of "all nations", because all three of these events are in different locations. Ezekiel's event is in the mountains and open fields, followed by burial in "The Valley of Hamongog" which is east of the Dead Sea and is *"the valley of the passengers on the east of the sea"*.[39]

> EZEKIEL 39
> 11 And it shall come to pass in that day, *that* I will give unto Gog a place there of graves in Israel, the valley of the passengers on the east of the sea: and it shall stop the *noses* of the passengers: and there shall they bury Gog and all his multitude: and they shall call *it* The valley of Hamongog.

Armageddon is the gathering place for battle at the foot of Mount Megiddo in the valley of Jezreel, north and west of Jerusalem.[40] The judgment of all nations is in the valley of Jehoshaphat which has several possible locations, with the most likely being the wilderness south of Jerusalem.[41]

> JOEL 3
> 2 I will also gather all nations, and will bring them down into the valley of Jehoshaphat, and will plead with them there for my people and *for* my heritage Israel, whom they have scattered among the nations, and parted my land.
> 12 Let the heathen be wakened, and come up to the valley of Jehoshaphat: for there will I sit to judge all the heathen round about.

Gog and Magog, Armageddon, and nation judgment are basically in different locations. Gog/Magog and Armageddon are both "fought" by GOD, with there being no evidence of Israel doing any fighting nor attempting any self-protection. After Armageddon, judgment is of all nations, not only Gog and Magog.

There are statements through Ezekiel that nations, heathens, and Israel "shall know that I am the Lord":

> EZEKIEL 38
> 16 And thou shalt come up against my people of Israel, as a cloud to cover the land; it shall be in the latter days, and I will bring thee against my land, that the heathen

may know me, when I shall be sanctified in thee, 0 Gog, before their eyes.

EZEKIEL 39
[6] And I will send a fire on Magog, and among them that dwell carelessly in the isles: and they shall know that I *am* the LORD.
[7] So will I make my holy name known in the midst of my people Israel; and I will not *let them* pollute my holy name any more: and the heathen shall know that *I am* the LORD, the Holy One in Israel.
[28] Then shall they know that *I am* the LORD their God, which caused them to be led into captivity among the heathen: but I have gathered them unto their own land, and have left none of them any more there.

However, Ezekiel also contains two statements indicating not all "nations will know the Lord" (*many* instead of *all*), and this would show the Gog and Magog event occurs prior to Armageddon:

EZEKIEL 38
[23] Thus will I magnify myself, and sanctify myself; and I will be known in the eyes of many nations, and they shall know that I *am* the LORD.

EZEKIEL 39
[27] When I have brought them again from the people, and gathered them out of their enemies' lands, and am sanctified in them in the sight of many nations;

Gog and Magog being destroyed supernaturally by GOD results in Israel, some heathens and some nations recognizing the Lord's actions on behalf of Israel. **This would set the stage for Israel to commence worship, festivals and sacrifices!**

In the Olivet Discourse, Jesus Christ stated:

MATTHEW 24
[6] And ye shall hear of wars and rumours of wars: see that ye be not troubled: for all *these things* must come to pass, but the end is not yet.

> 7 For nation shall rise against nation, and kingdom against kingdom: and there shall be famines, and pestilences, and earthquakes, in divers places.

It is suggested that the Gog and Magog episode will be part of "nation shall rise against nation, and kingdom against kingdom". With general world recognition that Israel had been supernaturally protected by GOD (the GOD of Israel), the world is likely to recognize Israel's GOD as the true GOD. Covenant confirmation would be a natural result to allow Israel's sacrifices and worship.

Jesus Christ will not be recognized as Deity by the world, nor Israel, until the resurrection and Rapture:

> REVELATION 1
> 7 Behold, he cometh with clouds; and every eye shall see him, and they *also* which pierced him: and all kindreds of the earth shall wail because of him. Even so, Amen.

"When Gog shall come against the land of Israel . . . every man's sword shall be against his brother" (Ezek. 38:18, 21). "The Second Seal will take peace from the earth and that they should kill one another" (Rev. 6:3–4). "Nation shall rise against nation, and kingdom against kingdom" (Luke 21:10). "But before all these, they shall lay their hands on you, and persecute you, . . . for my name's sake" (Luke 21:12).

Wars, people, and nations/kingdoms fighting among themselves, persecutions of believers in Jesus Christ and GOD's protection of Israel should precede covenant confirmation.

43. What to Do?

The idea, or recognition, that Believers will experience years of man's and Satan's wrath can be very disturbing. I know, I experience it. However, I also know there is only one answer: faith and trust in Lord Jesus Christ! The more prayer, time and study that are directed to God and His Scripture, the more faith, hope and love grow and grow. Thank God!

The Word through God's Anointed

Ecclesiastes 8
6 Because to every purpose there is time and judgment,
therefore the misery of man *is* great upon him.
7 For he knoweth not that which shall be: for who can tell
him when it shall be?
8 *There is* no man that hath power over the spirit to retain
the spirit; neither *hath he* power in the day of death: and
there is no discharge in *that* war; neither shall wickedness
deliver those that are given to it.

Psalm 18
2 The Lord *is* my rock, and my fortress, and my deliverer;
my God, my strength, in whom I will trust; my buckler,
and the horn of my salvation, *and* my high tower.
3 I will call upon the Lord, *who is worthy* to be praised: so
shall I be saved from mine enemies.
21 For I have kept the ways of the Lord, and have not
wickedly departed from my God.
27 For thou wilt save the afflicted people; but wilt bring
down high looks.
30 *As for* God, his way *is* perfect: the word of the Lord is
tried: he *is* a buckler to all those that trust in him.

The Word through God's Apostles

I Peter 4
12 Beloved, think it not strange concerning the fiery trial
which is to try you, as though some strange thing happened
unto you:
13 But rejoice, inasmuch as ye are partakers of Christ's
sufferings; that, when his glory shall be revealed, ye may
be glad also with exceeding joy.
16 Yet if *any man suffer* as a Christian, let him not be ashamed;
but let him glorify God on this behalf.

17 For the time *is come* that judgment must begin at the house of God: and if *it* first *begin* at us, what shall the end *be* of them that obey not the gospel of God?
18 And if the righteous scarcely be saved, where shall the ungodly and the sinner appear?
19 Wherefore let them that suffer according to the will of God commit the keeping of their souls *to him* in well doing, as unto a faithful Creator.

HEBREWS 13
5 *Let your* conversation *be* without covetousness; *and be* content with such things as ye have: for he hath said, I will never leave thee, nor forsake thee.
6 So that we may boldly say, The Lord *is* my helper, and I will not fear what man shall do unto me.

I JOHN 3
2 Beloved now are we the sons of God, and it doth not yet appear what we shall be: but we know that, when he shall appear, we shall be like him; for we shall see him as he is.
3 And every man that hath this hope in him purifieth himself, even as he is pure.

I JOHN 5
4 For whatsoever is born of God overcometh the world: and this is the victory that overcometh the world, *even* our faith.

The Word through GOD's Son, Lord Jesus Christ

JOHN 14
1 Let not your heart be troubled: ye believe in God, believe also in me.
2 In my Father's house are many mansions: if *it were* not *so,* I would have told you. I go to prepare a place for you.
3 And if I go and prepare a place for you, I will come again, and receive you unto myself; that where I am, *there* ye may be also.

MATTHEW 6
34 Take therefore no thought for the morrow: for the morrow shall take thought for the things of itself. Sufficient unto the day *is* the evil thereof.

LUKE 12
4 And I say unto you my friends, Be not afraid of them that kill the body, and after that have no more that they can do.
8 Also I say unto you, Whosoever shall confess me before men, him shall the Son of man also confess before the angels of God:
22 And he said unto his disciples, Therefore I say unto you, Take no thought for your life, what ye shall eat; neither for the body, what ye shall put on.
30 For all these things do the nations of the world seek after: and your Father knoweth that ye have need of these things.
32 Fear not, little flock; for it is your Father's good pleasure to give you the kingdom.
36 And ye yourselves like unto men that wait for their lord, when he will return from the wedding; that when he cometh and knocketh, they may open unto him immediately.
37 Blessed *are* those servants, whom the lord when he cometh shall find watching: verily I say unto you, that he shall gird himself, and make them to sit down to meat, and will come forth and serve them.

And, Last but Not Least

REVELATION 22
21 **The grace of our Lord Jesus Christ *be* with you all. Amen.**

Appendix

<u>All</u> uses of Greek word #3880 (*Take/Receive*)

Matthew
1:20: Joseph . . . <u>take</u> . . . thee Mary thy wife
1:24: Joseph . . . <u>took unto</u> him his wife
2:13: Joseph . . . <u>take</u> . . . child and his mother . . . flee
2:14: he <u>took</u> . . . child . . . mother . . . into . . . Egypt:
2:20: <u>take</u> . . . child and his mother . . . into . . . Israel:
2:21: <u>took</u> . . . child and his mother . . . into Israel.
4:5: <u>taketh</u> him up [*him* is Jesus]
4:8: <u>taketh</u> him up [*him* is Jesus]
17:1: Jesus <u>taketh</u> Peter, James . . . into . . . mountain
18:16: <u>take</u> . . . one or two more . . . witnesses [Jesus talking to *disciples,* (*verse* 1)]
20:17: Jesus . . . <u>took</u> the twelve disciples
26:37: he <u>took</u> with him Peter . . . [*he* is Jesus]
27:27: soldiers . . . <u>took</u> Jesus into . . . hall

Mark
4:36: they <u>took</u> him . . . in . . . ship . . . [*him* is Jesus]
5:40: he <u>taketh</u> the father . . . mother . . . [*he* is Jesus]
7:4: they <u>received</u> to hold . . . [*they* are Pharisees/Scribes]
9:2: Jesus <u>taketh</u> Peter, and James, and John
10:32: he <u>took</u> . . . the twelve . . . to tell them . . . [*he* is Jesus]
14:33: he <u>taketh</u> . . . Peter and James and John . . . [*he* is Jesus]

Luke
9:10: apostles . . . he <u>took</u> them . . . privately . . . [*he* is Jesus]
9:28: he <u>took</u> Peter and James and John . . . mountain . . . [*he* is Jesus]
18:31: he <u>took</u> . . . the twelve, and said . . . [*he* is Jesus]

John
1:11: his own <u>received</u> him not. [*his/him* is Jesus]
14:3: I . . . <u>receive</u> you unto myself . . . [*I/myself* is Jesus]
19:16: they <u>took</u> Jesus, and led him away.

There are two instances where the *taken* ones and the one *taking* are evil spirits; however, it was for their benefit:

1. **Matthew**
   12:45: <u>taketh</u> with himself seven other spirits

2. **Luke**
   11:26: goeth he, and taketh . . . other spirits

Acts
15:39: Barnabas took Mark
16:33: he took them . . . baptized . . . [*he* is a guard: *them* his family]
21:24: Them take, and purify thyself . . . [*thyself* is Paul]
21:26: Paul took the men
21:23: Who . . . took soldier . . . left beating of Paul [*Who* is captain]
23:18: he took him . . . [centurion took Paul for protection]

I Corinthians
11:23: I have received of the Lord . . . [*I* is Paul]
15:1: gospel . . . which also ye have received
15:3: which I also received . . . [Paul received gospel]

Galatians
1:9: gospel . . . ye have received
1:12: received . . . the Revelation of Jesus Christ.

Philippians
4:9: things . . . received . . . God . . . with you.

Colossians
2:6: ye . . . received Christ Jesus the Lord
4:17: ministry . . . received in the Lord

I Thessalonians
2:13: ye received . . . please God
4:1: ye have received . . . please God

II Thessalonians
3:6: tradition . . . received of us. [*us* indicates Paul]

Hebrews
12:28: we receiving a kingdom . . . may serve God

After understanding the usage of the word #3880, there can be no justification in assuming *taken* is directed to *wicked* individuals. *Taken* refers to Believers.

Matthew
24:40: two . . . in the field . . . one . . . taken . . . other left.
24:41: Two . . . grinding . . . one . . . taken . . . other left.

Luke
17:34: two . . . in . . . bed . . . one . . . taken . . . other left.
17:35: Two . . . grinding . . . one . . . taken . . . other left.
17:36: Two . . . in . . . field . . . one . . . taken . . . other left.

References

1. *Rapture: Post Tribulation and Pre-Wrath* is intended to be doctrinal and there is no desire to identify organizations, denominations nor individuals. Reference #1 will be identified if requested in writing with appropriate justification.
2. Rosenthal, Marvin J.: *The Pre-Wrath Rapture of the Church*, 1990, Thomas Nelson, Inc., Publishers, pgs. 256–261.
3. VanKampen, Robert: *The Sign*, 1992, 1993, Crossway Books, a division of Good News Publishers, pgs,207–210, 488–490.
4. VanKampen, Robert: *The Rapture Question Answered*, 1997, Fleming H. Revell, a division of Baker Book House Company, pgs. 123–125.
5. Marshall, Paul with Gilbert, Lela: *Their Blood Cries Out*, copyright 1997, Word Publishing, Nashville, Tennessee. All rights reserved. Used by permission, pg. 160.
6. Young, Robert: *Youngs Analytical Concordance to the Bible*, 1982, Thomas Nelson Publishers, pg. 804 & Index-Lexicon to the New Testament, pg. 84 (#4035).
7. Strong, James: *The New Strong's Exhaustive Concordance of the Bible*, 1984, Thomas Nelson Publishers, pg. 868 & *Dictionary of the Greek Testament* pg. 57 (#4035).
8. Vine, W. E. & Unger, M. F. & White, W.: *An Expository Dictionary of Biblical Words*, 1984, *New Testament Words*, pg. 945.
9. Strong: *Greek Dictionary of the New Testament*, pg. 52 (#3700).
10. Zodiates, Spiros: *The Complete Word Study Dictionary*, 1993, AMG Publishers, pg. 908 (#1492).
11. Vine: pgs. 562, 563.
12. Ibid., pg. 129.
13. (Same situation as Reference#1)
14. Vine: pg. 1270.
15. Strong: Appendix to the Main Concordance, pg. 21 (#575).
16. Young: pg. 376.
17. Strong: pgs. 595–596 (#1492).
18. Young: pg. 578.

19. Vine: pg. 628.
20. Byers, Marvin: *The Final Victory: The Year 2000*, 1994, Treasure House, pgs. 126–131, 153–160, 167–187.
21. Showers, Renald E.: *The Most High God*, 1982, *The Friends of Israel Gospel Ministry*, pgs. 120–127.
22. Ibid., pgs. 162–163.
23. Walvoord, John F.: *The Bible Knowledge Commentary*, Vol. 1 (O.T.), Victor Books, pg. 1369.
24. Byers: pgs. 287–288.
25. Strong: *Greek Dictionary of the New Testament*, pg. 70 (#4969).
26. Vine: pg. 268.
27. Ibid., pg. 868.
28. Zodhiates, Spiros: *The Hebrew-Greek Key Study Bible*, 1984, Baker Book House, pg. 1689–1690 (#1849), pgs. 1689–1690 (#1849).
29. McGee, J. Vernon: *Revelation* , Vol. I, 1981, Thru the Bible Books, pgs. 73–76.
30. Zodhiates, Spiros: *The Hebrew-Greek Key Study Bible*, 1984, Baker Book House, pg. 1601 (#3617).
31. Young: pg. 490.
32. Zodhiates: pg. 1650 (#8267).
33. Taylor, Charles R.: *Those Who Remain*, 1980, Today in Bible Prophecy, Inc., pgs. 35–38.
34. Vine: *Nelson's Expository Dictionary of the Old Testament*, pgs. 472–473.
35. Strong: *Dictionary of the Hebrew Bible*, pg. 63 (#4178).
36. Zodhiates: pg. 1598 (#3372).
37. Strong: *Dictionary of the Hebrew Bible*, pg. 19 (#958).
38. Zodhiates: pg. 1650 (#8252).
39. Pfeiffer, C. F., et al, Editors: *Wycliffe Bible Encyclopedia*, Moody Press, 1975, Vol. I, pg. 748.
40. Bryant, T. Alton, Editor: *The New Compact Bible Dictionary*, 1967, Zondervan Publishing House, pg. 55.
41. Pfeiffer: *Wycliffe Bible Encyclopedia*, Vol. I, pg. 890.